CRAFTSMANSHIP IN TEACHING

First published 1912
This edition published by Lector House in 2024

ISBN: 978-93-6138-984-9

Lector House LLP
Registered Office: H. No. 96, Block C, Tomar Colony,
Burari, Delhi – 110084, India
info@lectorhouse.com
www.lectorhouse.com

CRAFTSMANSHIP IN TEACHING

WILLIAM CHANDLER BAGLEY

2024

LECTOR HOUSE LLP

CRAFTSMANSHIP IN TEACHING

BY

WILLIAM CHANDLER BAGLEY

AUTHOR OF
"THE EDUCATIVE PROCESS," "CLASSROOM MANAGEMENT,"
"EDUCATIONAL VALUES," ETC.

TO MY PARENTS

PREFACE

The following papers are published chiefly because they treat in a concrete and personal manner some of the principles which the writer has developed in two previously published books, *The Educative Process* and *Classroom Management,* and in a forthcoming volume, *Educational Values*. It is hoped that the more informal discussions presented in the following pages will, in some slight measure, supplement the theoretical and systematic treatment which necessarily characterizes the other books. In this connection, it should be stated that the materials of the first paper here presented were drawn upon in writing Chapter XVIII of *Classroom Management,* and that the second paper simply states in a different form the conclusions reached in Chapter I of *The Educative Process*.

The writer is indebted to his colleague, Professor L.F. Anderson, for many criticisms and suggestions and to Miss Bernice Harrison for invaluable aid in editing the papers for publication. But his heaviest debt, here as elsewhere, is to his wife, to whose encouraging sympathy and inspiration whatever may be valuable in this or in his other books must be largely attributed.

URBANA, ILLINOIS,
MARCH 1, 1911

CONTENTS

CRAFTSMANSHIP IN TEACHING

CHAPTER I

CRAFTSMANSHIP IN TEACHING[1]

I

> "In the laboratory of life, each newcomer repeats the old experiments, and laughs and weeps for himself. We will be explorers, though all the highways have their guideposts and every bypath is mapped. Helen of Troy will not deter us, nor the wounds of Cæsar frighten, nor the voice of the king crying 'Vanity!' from his throne dismay. What wonder that the stars that once sang for joy are dumb and the constellations go down in silence."—ARTHUR SHERBURNE HARDY: *The Wind of Destiny*.

We tend, I think, to look upon the advice that we give to young people as something that shall disillusionize them. The cynic of forty sneers at what he terms the platitudes of commencement addresses. He knows life. He has been behind the curtains. He has looked upon the other side of the scenery,—the side that is just framework and bare canvas. He has seen the ugly machinery that shifts the stage setting—the stage setting which appears so impressive when viewed from the front. He has seen the rouge on the cheeks that seem to blush with the bloom of youth and beauty and innocence, and has caught the cold glint in the eyes that, from the distance, seem to languish with tenderness and love. Why, he asks, should we create an illusion that must thus be rudely dispelled? Why revamp and refurbish the old platitudes and dole them out each succeeding year? Why not tell these young people the truth and let them be prepared for the fate that must come sooner or later?

But the cynic forgets that there are some people who never lose their illusions,—some men and women who are always young,—and, whatever may be the type of men and women that other callings and professions desire to enroll in their service, this is the type that education needs. The great problem of the teacher is to keep himself in this class, to keep himself young, to preserve the very things that the cynic pleases to call the illusions of his youth. And so much do I desire to impress these novitiates into our calling with the necessity for preserving their ideals

[1] An address to the graduating class of the Oswego, New York, State Normal School, February, 1907.

that I shall ask them this evening to consider with me some things which would, I fear, strike the cynic as most illusionary and impractical. The initiation ceremonies that admitted the young man to the privileges and duties of knighthood included the taking of certain vows, the making of certain pledges of devotion and fidelity to the fundamental principles for which chivalry stood. And I should like this evening to imagine that these graduates are undergoing an analogous initiation into the privileges and duties of schoolcraft, and that these vows which I shall enumerate, embody some of the ideals that govern the work of that craft.

II

And the first of these vows I shall call, for want of a better term, the vow of "artistry,"—the pledge that the initiate takes to do the work that his hand finds to do in the best possible manner, without reference to the effort that it may cost or to the reward that it may or may not bring.

I call this the vow of artistry because it represents the essential attitude of the artist toward his work. The cynic tells us that ideals are illusions of youth, and yet, the other day I saw expressed in a middle-aged working-man a type of idealism that is not at all uncommon in this world. He was a house painter; his task was simply the prosaic job of painting a door; and yet, from the pains which he took with that work, an observer would have concluded that it was, to the painter, the most important task in the world. And that, after all, is the true test of craft artistry: to the true craftsman the work that he is doing must be the most important thing that can be done. One of the best teachers that I know is that kind of a craftsman in education. A student was once sent to observe his work. He was giving a lesson upon the "attribute complement" to an eighth-grade grammar class. I asked the student afterward what she had got from her visit. "Why," she replied, "that man taught as if the very greatest achievement in life would be to get his pupils to understand the attribute complement,—and when he had finished, they did understand it."

In a narrower sense, this vow of artistry carries with it an appreciation of the value of technique. From the very fact of their normal school training, these graduates already possess a certain measure of skill, a certain mastery of the technique of their craft. This initial mastery has been gained in actual contact with the problems of school work in their practice teaching. They have learned some of the rudiments; they have met and mastered some of the rougher, cruder difficulties. The finer skill, the delicate and intangible points of technique, they must acquire, as all beginners must acquire them, through the strenuous processes of self-discipline in the actual work of the years that are to come. This is a process that takes time, energy, constant and persistent application. All that this school or any school can do for its students in this respect is to start them upon the right track in the acquisition of skill. But do not make the mistake of assuming that this is a small and unimportant matter. If this school did nothing more than this, it would still repay tenfold the cost of its establishment and maintenance. Three fourths of the failures in a world that sometimes seems full of failures are due to nothing more nor less than a wrong start. In spite of the growth of professional training for teachers within the past fifty years, many of our lower schools are still filled with raw recruits, fresh from the high schools and even from the grades, who must learn every practical lesson of teaching through the medium of their own mistakes. Even if this were all, the process would involve a tremendous and uncalled-for waste. But this is not all; for, out of this multitude of untrained teachers, only a small proportion ever recognize the mistakes that they make and try to correct them.

To you who are beginning the work of life, the mastery of technique may seem a comparatively unimportant matter. You recognize its necessity, of course, but you think of it as something of a mechanical nature,—an integral part of the day's work, but uninviting in itself,—something to be reduced as rapidly as possible to the plane of automatism and dismissed from the mind. I believe that you will outgrow this notion. As you go on with your work, as you increase in skill, ever and ever the fascination of its technique will take a stronger and stronger hold upon you. This is the great saving principle of our workaday life. This is the factor that keeps the toiler free from the deadening effects of mechanical routine. It is the factor that keeps the farmer at his plow, the artisan at his bench, the lawyer at his desk, the artist at his palette.

I once worked for a man who had accumulated a large fortune. At the age of seventy-five he divided this fortune among his children, intending to retire; but he could find pleasure and comfort only in the routine of business. In six months he was back in his office. He borrowed twenty-five thousand dollars on his past reputation and started in to have some fun. I was his only employee at the time, and I sat across the big double desk from him, writing his letters and keeping his accounts. He would sit for hours, planning for the establishment of some industry or running out the lines that would entangle some old adversary. I did not stay with him very long, but before I left, he had a half-dozen thriving industries on his hands, and when he died three years later he had accumulated another fortune of over a million dollars.

That is an example of what I mean by the fascination that the technique of one's craft may come to possess. It is the joy of doing well the work that you know how to do. The finer points of technique,—those little things that seem so trivial in themselves and yet which mean everything to skill and efficiency,—what pride the competent artisan or the master artist takes in these! How he delights to revel in the jargon of his craft! How he prides himself in possessing the knowledge and the technical skill that are denied the layman!

I am aware that I am somewhat unorthodox in urging this view of your work upon you. Teachers have been encouraged to believe that details are not only unimportant but stultifying,—that teaching ability is a function of personality, and not a product of a technique that must be acquired through the strenuous discipline of experience. One of the most skillful teachers of my acquaintance is a woman down in the grades. I have watched her work for days at a time, striving to learn its secret. I can find nothing there that is due to genius,—unless we accept George Eliot's definition of genius as an infinite capacity for receiving discipline. That teacher's success, by her own statement, is due to a mastery of technique, gained through successive years of growth checked by a rigid responsibility for results.

She has found out by repeated trial how to do her work in the best way; she has discovered the attitude toward her pupils that will get the best work from them,—the clearest methods of presenting subject matter; the most effective ways in which to drill; how to use text-books and make study periods issue in something besides mischief; and, more than all else, how to do these things without losing sight of the true end of education. Very frequently I have taken visiting school men to see this teacher's work. Invariably after leaving her room they have turned to me with such expressions as these: "A born teacher!" "What interest!" "What a personality!" "What a voice!"—everything, in fact, except this,—which would have been the truth: "What a tribute to years of effort and struggle and self-discipline!"

I have a theory which I have never exploited very seriously, but I will give it to you for what it is worth. It is this: elementary education especially needs a literary interpretation. It needs a literary artist who will portray to the public in the form of fiction the real life of the elementary school,—who will idealize the technique of teaching as Kipling idealized the technique of the marine engineer, as Balzac idealized the technique of the journalist, as Du Maurier and a hundred other novelists have idealized the technique of the artist. We need some one to exploit our shop-talk on the reading public, and to show up our work as you and I know it, not as you and I have been told by laymen that it ought to be,—a literature of the elementary school with the cant and the platitudes and the goody-goodyism left out, and in their place something of the virility, of the serious study, of the manful effort to solve difficult problems, of the real and vital achievements that are characteristic of thousands of elementary schools throughout the country to-day.

At first you will be fascinated by the novelty of your work. But that soon passes away. Then comes the struggle,—then comes the period, be it long or short, when you will work with your eyes upon the clock, when you will count the weeks, the days, the hours, the minutes that lie between you and vacation time. Then will be the need for all the strength and all the energy that you can summon to your aid. Fail here, and your fate is decided once and for all. If, in your work, you never get beyond this stage, you will never become the true craftsman. You will never taste the joy that is vouchsafed the expert, the efficient craftsman.

The length of this period varies with different individuals. Some teachers "find themselves" quickly. They seem to settle at once into the teaching attitude. With others is a long, uphill fight. But it is safe to say that if, at the end of three years, your eyes still habitually seek the clock,—if, at the end of that time, your chief reward is the check that comes at the end of every fourth week,—then your doom is sealed.

III

And the second vow that I should urge these graduates to take is the vow of fidelity to the spirit of their calling. We have heard a great deal in recent years about making education a profession. I do not like that term myself. Education is not a profession in the sense that medicine and law are professions. It is rather a craft, for its duty is to produce, to mold, to fashion, to transform a certain raw material into a useful product. And, like all crafts, education must possess the craft spirit. It must have a certain code of craft ethics; it must have certain standards of craft excellence and efficiency. And in these the normal school must instruct its students, and to these it should secure their pledge of loyalty and fidelity and devotion.

A true conception of this craft spirit in education is one of the most priceless possessions of the young teacher, for it will fortify him against every criticism to which his calling is subjected. It is revealing no secret to tell you that the teacher's work is not held in the highest regard by the vast majority of men and women in other walks of life. I shall not stop to inquire why this is so, but the fact cannot be doubted, and every now and again some incident of life, trifling perhaps in itself, will bring it to your notice; but most of all, perhaps you will be vexed and incensed by the very thing that is meant to put you at your ease—the patronizing attitude which your friends in other walks of life will assume toward you and toward your work.

When will the good public cease to insult the teacher's calling with empty flattery? When will men who would never for a moment encourage their own sons to enter the work of the public schools, cease to tell us that education is the greatest and noblest of all human callings? Education does not need these compliments. The teacher does not need them. If he is a master of his craft, he knows what education means,—he knows this far better than any layman can tell him. And what boots it to him, if, with all this cant and hypocrisy about the dignity and worth of his calling, he can sometimes hold his position only at the sacrifice of his self-respect?

But what is the relation of the craft spirit to these facts? Simply this: the true craftsman, by the very fact that he is a true craftsman, is immune to these influences. What does the true artist care for the plaudits or the sneers of the crowd? True, he seeks commendation and welcomes applause, for your real artist is usually extremely human; but he seeks this commendation from another source—from a source that metes it out less lavishly and yet with unconditioned candor. He seeks the commendation of his fellow-workmen, the applause of "those who know, and always will know, and always will understand." He plays to the pit and not to the gallery, for he knows that when the pit really approves the gallery will often echo and reëcho the applause, albeit it has not the slightest conception of what the whole thing is about.

What education stands in need of to-day is just this: a stimulating and pervasive craft spirit. If a human calling would win the world's respect, it must first respect itself; and the more thoroughly it respects itself, the greater will be the measure of homage that the world accords it. In one of the educational journals a few years ago, the editors ran a series of articles under the general caption, "Why I am a teacher." It reminded me of the spirited discussion that one of the Sunday papers started some years since on the world-old query, "Is marriage a failure?" And some of the articles were fully as sickening in their harrowing details as were some of the whining matrimonial confessions of the latter series. But the point that I wish to make is this: your true craftsman in education never stops to ask himself such questions. There are some men to whom schoolcraft is a mistress. They love it, and their devotion is no make-believe, fashioned out of sentiment, and donned for the purpose of hiding inefficiency or native indolence. They love it as some men love Art, and others Business, and others War. They do not stop to ask the reason why, to count the cost, or to care a fig what people think. They are properly jealous of their special knowledge, gained through years of special study; they are justly jealous of their special skill gained through years of discipline and training. They resent the interference of laymen in matters purely professional. They resent such interference as would a reputable physician, a reputable lawyer, a reputable engineer. They resent officious patronage and "fussy" meddling. They resent all these things manfully, vigorously. But your true craftsman will not whine. If the conditions under which he works do not suit him, he will fight for their betterment, but he will not whine.

IV

And yet this vow of fidelity and devotion to the spirit of schoolcraft would be an empty form without the two complementary vows that give it worth and meaning. These are the vow of poverty and the vow of service. It is through these that the true craft spirit must find its most vigorous expression and its only justification. The very corner stone of schoolcraft is service, and one fundamental lesson that the tyro in schoolcraft must learn, especially in this materialistic age, is that the value of service is not to be measured in dollars and cents. In this respect, teaching resembles art, music, literature, discovery, invention, and pure science; for, if all the workers in all of these branches of human activity got together and demanded of the world the real fruits of their self-sacrifice and labor,—if they demanded all the riches and comforts and amenities of life that have flowed directly or indirectly from their efforts,—there would be little left for the rest of mankind. Each of these activities is represented by a craft spirit that recognizes this great truth. The artist or the scientist who has an itching palm, who prostitutes his craft for the sake of worldly gain, is quickly relegated to the oblivion that he deserves. He loses caste, and the caste of craft is more precious to your true craftsman than all the gold of the modern Midas.

You may think that this is all very well to talk about, but that it bears little agreement to the real conditions. Let me tell you that you are mistaken. Go ask Röntgen why he did not keep the X-rays a secret to be exploited for his own personal gain. Ask the shade of the great Helmholtz why he did not patent the ophthalmoscope. Go to the University of Wisconsin and ask Professor Babcock why he gave to the world without money and without price the Babcock test—an invention which is estimated to mean more than one million dollars every year to the farmers and dairymen of that state alone. Ask the men on the geological survey who laid bare the great gold deposits of Alaska why they did not leave a thankless and ill-paid service to acquire the wealth that lay at their feet. Because commercialized ideals govern the world that we know, we think that all men's eyes are jaundiced, and that all men's vision is circumscribed by the milled rim of the almighty dollar. But we are sadly, miserably mistaken.

Do you think that these ideals of service from which every taint of self-seeking and commercialism have been eliminated—do you think that these are mere figments of the impractical imagination? Go ask Perry Holden out in Iowa. Go ask Luther Burbank out in California. Go to any agricultural college in this broad land and ask the scientists who are doing more than all other forces combined to increase the wealth of the people. Go to the scientific departments at Washington where men of genius are toiling for a pittance. Ask them how much of the wealth for which they are responsible they propose to put into their own pockets. What will be their answer? They will tell you that all they ask is a living wage, a chance to work, and the just recognition of their services by those who know and appreciate and understand.

But let me hasten to add that these men claim no especial merit for their altruism and unselfishness. They do not pose before the world as philanthropists. They do not strut about and preen themselves as who would say: "See what a noble man am I! See how I sacrifice myself for the welfare of society!" The attitude of cant and pose is entirely alien to the spirit of true service. Their delight is in doing, in serving, in producing. But beyond this, they have the faults and frailties of their kind,—save one,—the sin of covetousness. And again, all that they ask of the world is a living wage, and the privilege to serve.

And that is all that the true craftsman in education asks. The man or woman with the itching palm has no place in the schoolroom,—no place in any craft whose keynote is service. It is true that the teacher does not receive to-day, in all parts of our country, a living wage; and it is equally true that society at large is the greatest sufferer because of its penurious policy in this regard. I should applaud and support every movement that has for its purpose the raising of teachers' salaries to the level of those paid in other branches of professional service. Society should do this for its own benefit and in its own defense, not as a matter of charity to the men and women who, among all public servants, should be the last to be accused of feeding gratuitously at the public crib. I should approve all honest efforts of school men and school women toward this much-desired end. But whenever men and women enter schoolcraft because of the material rewards that it offers, the virtue will have gone out of our calling,—just as the virtue went out of the Church when, during the Middle Ages, the Church attracted men, not because of the opportunities that it offered for social service, but because of the opportunities that it offered for the acquisition of wealth and temporal power,—just as the virtue has gone out of certain other once-noble professions that have commercialized their standards and tarnished their ideals.

This is not to say that one condemns the man who devotes his life to the accumulation of property. The tremendous strides that our country has made in material civilization have been conditioned in part by this type of genius. Creative genius must always compel our admiration and our respect. It may create a world epic, a matchless symphony of tones or pigments, a scientific theory of tremendous grasp and limitless scope; or it may create a vast industrial system, a commercial enterprise of gigantic proportions, a powerful organization of capital. Genius is pretty much the same wherever we find it, and everywhere we of the common clay must recognize its worth.

The grave defect in our American life is not that we are hero worshipers, but rather that we worship but one type of hero; we recognize but one type of achievement; we see but one sort of genius. For two generations our youth have been led to believe that there is only one ambition that is worth while,—the ambition of property. Success at any price is the ideal that has been held up before our boys and girls. And to-day we are reaping the rewards of this distorted and unjust view of life.

I recently met a man who had lived for some years in the neighborhood of St. Paul and Minneapolis,—a section that is peopled, as you know, very largely by Scandinavian immigrants and their descendants. This man told me that he had been particularly impressed by the high idealism of the Norwegian people. His business brought him in contact with Norwegian immigrants in what are called the lower walks of life,—with workingmen and servant girls,—and he made it a point to ask each of these young men and young women the same question. "Tell me," he would say, "who are the great men of your country? Who are the men toward whom the youth of your land are led to look for inspiration? Who are the men whom your boys are led to imitate and emulate and admire?" And he said that he almost always received the same answer to this question: the great names of the Norwegian nation that had been burned upon the minds even of these workingmen and servant girls were just four in number: Ole Bull, Björnson, Ibsen, Nansen. Over and over again he asked that same question; over and over again he received the same answer: Ole Bull, Björnson, Ibsen, Nansen. A great musician, a great novelist, a great dramatist, a great scientist.

And I conjectured as I heard of this incident, What would be the answer if the youth of our land were asked that question: "Who are the great men of *your* country? What type of achievement have you been led to imitate and emulate and admire?" How many of our boys and girls have even heard of our great men in the world of culture,—unless, indeed, such men lived a half century ago and have got into the school readers by this time? How many of our boys and girls have ever heard of MacDowell, or James, or Whistler, or Sargent?

I have said that the teacher must take the vow of service. What does this imply except that the opportunity for service, the privilege of serving, should be the opportunity that one seeks, and that the achievements toward which one aspires should be the achievements of serving? The keynote of service lies in self-sacrifice,—in self-forgetfulness, rather,—in merging one's own life in the lives of others. The attitude of the true teacher in this respect is very similar to the attitude of the true parent. In so far as the parent feels himself responsible for the character of his children, in so far as he holds himself culpable for their shortcomings and instrumental in shaping their virtues, he loses himself in his children. What we term parental affection is, I believe, in part an outgrowth of this feeling of responsibility. The situation is precisely the same with the teacher. It is when the teacher begins to feel himself responsible for the growth and development of his pupils that he begins to find himself in the work of teaching. It is then that the effective devotion to his pupils has its birth. The affection that comes prior to this is, I think, very likely to be of the sentimental and transitory sort.

In education, as in life, we play altogether too carelessly with the word "love."

The test of true devotion is self-forgetfulness. Until the teacher reaches that point, he is conscious of two distinct elements in his work,—himself and his pupils. When that time comes, his own *ego* drops from view, and he lives in and for his pupils. The young teacher's tendency is always to ask himself, "Do my pupils like me?" Let me say that this is beside the question. It is not, from his standpoint, a matter of the pupils liking their teacher, but of the teacher liking his pupils. That, I take it, must be constantly the point of view. If you ask the other question first, you will be tempted to gain your end by means that are almost certain to prove fatal,—to bribe and pet and cajole and flatter, to resort to the dangerous expedient of playing to the gallery; but the liking that you get in this way is not worth the price that you pay for it. I should caution young teachers against the short-sighted educational theories that are in the air to-day, and that definitely recommend this attitude. They may sound sweet, but they are soft and sticky in practice. Better be guided by instinct than by "half-baked" theory. I have no disposition to criticize the attempts that have been made to rationalize educational practice, but a great deal of contemporary theory starts at the wrong end. It has failed to go to the sources of actual experience for its data. I know a father and mother who have brought up ten children successfully, and I may say that you could learn more about managing boys and girls from observing their methods than from a half-dozen prominent books on educational theory that I could name.

And so I repeat that the true test of the teacher's fidelity to this vow of service is the degree in which he loses himself in his pupils,—the degree in which he lives and toils and sacrifices for them just for the pure joy that it brings him. Once you have tasted this joy, no carping sneer of the cynic can cause you to lose faith in your calling. Material rewards sink into insignificance. You no longer work with your eyes upon the clock. The hours are all too short for the work that you would do. You are as light-hearted and as happy as a child,—for you have lost yourself to find yourself, and you have found yourself to lose yourself.

V

And the final vow that I would have these graduates take is the vow of idealism,—the pledge of fidelity and devotion to certain fundamental principles of life which it is the business of education carefully to cherish and nourish and transmit untarnished to each succeeding generation. These but formulate in another way what the vows that I have already discussed mean by implication. One is the ideal of social service, upon which education must, in the last analysis, rest its case. The second is the ideal of science,—the pledge of devotion to that persistent unwearying search after truth, of loyalty to the great principles of unbiased observation and unprejudiced experiment, of willingness to accept the truth and be governed by it, no matter how disagreeable it may be, no matter how roughly it may trample down our pet doctrines and our preconceived theories. The nineteenth century left us a glorious heritage in the great discoveries and inventions that science has established. These must not be lost to posterity; but far better lose them than lose the spirit of free inquiry, the spirit of untrammeled investigation, the noble devotion to truth for its own sake that made these discoveries and inventions possible.

It is these ideals that education must perpetuate, and if education is successfully to perpetuate them, the teacher must himself be filled with a spirit of devotion to the things that they represent. Science has triumphed over superstition and fraud and error. It is the teacher's duty to see to it that this triumph is permanent, that mankind does not again fall back into the black pit of ignorance and superstition.

And so it is the teacher's province to hold aloft the torch, to stand against the materialistic tendencies that would reduce all human standards to the common denominator of the dollar, to insist at all times and at all places that this nation of ours was founded upon idealism, and that, whatever may be the prevailing tendencies of the time, its children shall still learn to live "among the sunlit peaks." And if the teacher is imbued with this idealism, although his work may take him very close to Mother Earth, he may still lift his head above the fog and look the morning sun squarely in the face.

CHAPTER II

OPTIMISM IN TEACHING[2]

Although the month is March and not November, it is never unseasonable to count up the blessings for which it is well to be thankful. In fact, from the standpoint of education, the spring is perhaps the appropriate time to perform this very pleasant function. As if still further to emphasize the fact that education, like civilization, is an artificial thing, we have reversed the operations of Mother Nature: we sow our seed in the fall and cultivate our crops during the winter and reap our harvests in the spring. I may be pardoned, therefore, for making the theme of my discussion a brief review of the elements of growth and victory for which the educator of to-day may justly be grateful, with, perhaps, a few suggestions of what the next few years may reasonably be expected to bring forth.

And this course is all the more necessary because, I believe, the teaching profession is unduly prone to pessimism. One might think at first glance that the contrary would be true. We are surrounded on every side by youth. Youth is the material with which we constantly deal. Youth is buoyant, hopeful, exuberant; and yet, with this material constantly surrounding us, we frequently find the task wearisome and apparently hopeless. The reason is not far to seek. Youth is not only buoyant, it is unsophisticated, it is inexperienced, in many important particulars it is crude. Some of its tastes must necessarily, in our judgment, hark back to the primitive, to the barbaric. Ours is continually the task to civilize, to sophisticate, to refine this raw material. But, unfortunately for us, the effort that we put forth does not always bring results that we can see and weigh and measure. The hopefulness of our material is overshadowed not infrequently by its crudeness. We take each generation as it comes to us. We strive to lift it to the plane that civilized society has reached. We do our best and pass it on, mindful of the many inadequacies, perhaps of the many failures, in our work. We turn to the new generation that takes its place. We hope for better materials, but we find no improvement.

And so you and I reflect in our occasional moments of pessimism that generic situation which inheres in the very work that we do. The constantly accelerated progress of civilization lays constantly increasing burdens upon us. In some way or another we must accomplish the task. In some way or another we must lift the child to the level of society, and, as society is reaching a continually higher and higher level, so the distance through which the child must be raised is ever increased. We would like to think that all this progress in the race would come to

[2] An address before the Oswego, New York, County Council of Education, March 28, 1908.

mean that we should be able to take the child at a higher level; but you who deal with children know from experience the principle for which the biologist Weismann stands sponsor—the principle, namely, that acquired characteristics are not inherited; that whatever changes may be wrought during life in the brains and nerves and muscles of the present generation cannot be passed on to its successor save through the same laborious process of acquisition and training; that, however far the civilization of the race may progress, education, whose duty it is to conserve and transmit this civilization, must always begin with the "same old child."

This, I take it, is the deep-lying cause of the schoolmaster's pessimism. In our work we are constantly struggling against that same inertia which held the race in bondage for how many millenniums only the evolutionist can approximate a guess,—that inertia of the primitive, untutored mind which we to-day know as the mind of childhood, but which, for thousands of generations, was the only kind of a mind that man possessed. This inertia has been conquered at various times in the course of recorded history,—in Egypt and China and India, in Chaldea and Assyria, in Greece and Rome,—conquered only again to reassert itself and drive man back into barbarism. Now we of the Western world have conquered it, let us hope, for all time; for we of the Western world have discovered an effective method of holding it in abeyance, and this method is universal public education.

Let Germany close her public schools, and in two generations she will lapse back into the semi-darkness of medievalism; let her close both her public schools and her universities, and three generations will fetch her face to face with the Dark Ages; let her destroy her libraries and break into ruin all of her works of art, all of her existing triumphs of technical knowledge and skill, from which a few, self-tutored, might glean the wisdom that is every one's to-day, and Germany will soon become the home of a savage race, as it was in the days of Tacitus and Cæsar. Let Italy close her public schools, and Italy will become the same discordant jumble of petty states that it was a century ago,—again to await, this time perhaps for centuries or millenniums, another Garibaldi and Victor Emmanuel to work her regeneration. Let Japan close her public schools, and Japan in two generations will be a barbaric kingdom of the Shoguns, shorn of every vestige of power and prestige,—the easy victim of the machinations of Western diplomats. Let our country cease in its work of education, and these United States must needs pass through the reverse stages of their growth until another race of savages shall roam through the unbroken forest, now and then to reach the shores of ocean and gaze through the centuries, eastward, to catch a glimpse of the new Columbus. Like the moving pictures of the kinetoscope when the reels are reversed, is the picture that imagination can unroll if we grant the possibility of a lapse from civilization to savagery.

And so when we take the broader view, we quickly see that, in spite of our pessimism, we are doing something in the world. We are part of that machine which civilization has invented and is slowly perfecting to preserve itself. We may be a very small part, but, so long as the responsibility for a single child rests upon us, we are not an unimportant part. Society must reckon with you and me perhaps in an infinitesimal degree, but it must reckon with the institution which we represent as it reckons with no other institution that it has reared to subserve its needs.

In a certain sense these statements are platitudes. We have repeated them over and over again until the words have lost their tremendous significance. And it behooves us now and again to revive the old substance in a new form,—to come afresh to a self-consciousness of our function. It is not good for any man to hold a debased and inferior opinion of himself or of his work, and in the field of schoolcraft it is easy to fall into this self-depreciating habit of thought. We cannot hope that the general public will ever come to view our work in the true perspective that I have very briefly outlined. It would probably not be wise to promulgate publicly so pronounced an affirmation of our function and of our worth. The popular mind must think in concrete details rather than in comprehensive principles, when the subject of thought is a specialized vocation. You and I have crude ideas, no doubt, of the lawyer's function, of the physician's function, of the clergyman's function. Not less crude are their ideas of our function. Even when they patronize us by saying that our work is the noblest that any man or woman would engage in, they have but a vague and shadowy perception of its real significance. I doubt not that, with the majority of those who thus pat us verbally upon the back, the words that they use are words only. They do not envy us our privileges,—unless it is our summer vacations,—nor do they encourage their sons to enter service in our craft. The popular mind—the nontechnical mind,—must work in the concrete;—it must have visible evidences of power and influence before it pays homage to a man or to an institution.

Throughout the German empire the traveler is brought constantly face to face with the memorials that have been erected by a grateful people to the genius of the Iron Chancellor. Bismarck richly deserves the tribute that is paid to his memory, but a man to be honored in this way must exert a tangible and an obvious influence.

And yet, in a broader sense, the preëminence of Germany is due in far greater measure to two men whose names are not so frequently to be found inscribed upon towers and monuments. In the very midst of the havoc and devastation wrought by the Napoleon wars,—at the very moment when the German people seemed hopelessly crushed and defeated,—an intellect more penetrating than that of Bismarck grasped the logic of the situation. With the inspiration that comes with true insight, the philosopher Fichte issued his famous Addresses to the German people. With clear-cut argument couched in white-hot words, he drove home the great principle that lies at the basis of United Germany and upon the results of which Bismarck and Von Moltke and the first Emperor erected the splendid structure that to-day commands the admiration of the world. Fichte told the German people that their only hope lay in universal, public education. And the kingdom of Prussia—impoverished, bankrupt, war-ridden, and war-devastated—heard the plea. A great scheme that comprehended such an education was already at hand. It had fallen almost stillborn from the only kind of a mind that could have produced it,—a mind that was suffused with an overwhelming love for humanity and incomparably rich with the practical experiences of a primary schoolmaster. It had fallen from the mind of Pestalozzi, the Swiss reformer, who thus stands with Fichte as one of the vital factors in the development of Germany's educational supremacy.

The people's schools of Prussia, imbued with the enthusiasm of Fichte and Pestalozzi,[3] gave to Germany the tremendous advantage that enabled it so easily to overcome its hereditary foe, when, two generations later, the Franco-Prussian War was fought; for the *Volksschule* gave to Germany something that no other nation of that time possessed; namely, an educated proletariat, an intelligent common people. Bismarck knew this when he laid his cunning plans for the unification of German states that was to crown the brilliant series of victories beginning at Sedan and ending within the walls of Paris. William of Prussia knew it when, in the royal palace at Versailles, he accepted the crown that made him the first Emperor of United Germany. Von Moltke knew it when, at the capitulation of Paris, he was asked to whom the credit of the victory was due, and he replied, in the frank simplicity of the true soldier and the true hero, "The schoolmaster did it."

And yet Bismarck and Von Moltke and the Emperor are the heroes of Germany, and if Fichte and Pestalozzi are not forgotten, at least their memories are not cherished as are the memories of the more tangible and obvious heroes. Instinct lies deeply embedded in human nature and it is instinctive to think in the concrete. And so I repeat that we cannot expect the general public to share in the respect and veneration which you and I feel for our calling, for you and I are technicians in education, and we can see the process as a comprehensive whole. But our fellow men and women have their own interests and their own departments of technical knowledge and skill; they see the schoolhouse and the pupils' desks and the books and other various material symbols of our work,—they see these things and call them education; just as we see a freight train thundering across the viaduct or a steamer swinging out in the lake and call these things commerce. In both cases, the nontechnical mind associates the word with something concrete and tangible; in both cases, the technical mind associates the same word with an abstract process, comprehending a movement of vast proportions.

To compress such a movement—whether it be commerce or government or education—in a single conception requires a multitude of experiences involving actual adjustments with the materials involved; involving constant reflection upon hidden meanings, painful investigations into hidden causes, and mastery of a vast body of specialized knowledge which it takes years of study to digest and assimilate.

It is not every stevedore upon the docks, nor every stoker upon the steamers, nor every brakeman upon the railroads, who comprehends what commerce really means. It is not every banker's clerk who knows the meaning of business. It is not every petty holder of public office who knows what government really means. But this, at least, is true: in proportion as the worker knows the meaning of the work that he does,—in proportion as he sees it in its largest relations to society and to life,—his work is no longer the drudgery of routine toil. It becomes instead an intelligent process directed toward a definite goal. It has acquired that touch of artistry which, so far as human testimony goes, is the only pure and uncontaminated

[3] It should be added that the movement toward universal education in Germany owed much to the work of pre-Pestalozzian reformers,—especially Francke and Basedow.

source of human happiness.

And the chief blessing for which you and I should be thankful to-day is that this larger view of our calling has been vouchsafed to us as it has been vouchsafed no former generation of teachers. Education as the conventional prerogative of the rich,—as the garment which separated the higher from the lower classes of society,—this could scarcely be looked upon as a fascinating and uplifting ideal from which to derive hope and inspiration in the day's work; and yet this was the commonly accepted function of education for thousands of years, and the teachers who did the actual work of instruction could not but reflect in their attitude and bearing the servile character of the task that they performed. Education to fit the child to earn a better living, to command a higher wage,—- this myopic view of the function of the school could do but little to make the work of teaching anything but drudgery; and yet it is this narrow and materialistic view that has dominated our educational system to within a comparatively few years.

So silently and yet so insistently have our craft ideals been transformed in the last two decades that you and I are scarcely aware that our point of view has been changed and that we are looking upon our work from a much higher point of vantage and in a light entirely new. And yet this is the change that has been wrought. That education, in its widest meaning, is the sole conservator and transmitter of civilization to successive generations found expression as far back as Aristotle and Plato, and has been vaguely voiced at intervals down through the centuries; but its complete establishment came only as an indirect issue of the great scientific discoveries of the nineteenth century, and its application to the problems of practical schoolcraft and its dissemination through the rank and file of teachers awaited the dawn of the twentieth century. To-day we see expressions and indications of the new outlook upon every hand, in the greatly increased professional zeal that animates the teacher's calling; in the widespread movement among all civilized countries to raise the standards of teachers, to eliminate those candidates for service who have not subjected themselves to the discipline of special preparation; in the increased endowments and appropriations for schools and seminaries that prepare teachers; and, perhaps most strikingly at the present moment, in that concerted movement to organize into institutions of formal education, all of those branches of training which have, for years, been left to the chance operation of economic needs working through the crude and unorganized though often effective apprentice system. The contemporary fervor for industrial education is only one expression of this new view that, in the last analysis, the school must stand sponsor for the conservation and transmission of every valuable item of experience, every usable fact or principle, every tiniest perfected bit of technical skill, every significant ideal or prejudice, that the race has acquired at the cost of so much struggle and suffering and effort.

I repeat that this new vantage point from which to gain a comprehensive view of our calling has been attained only as an indirect result of the scientific investigations of the nineteenth century. We are wont to study the history of education from the work and writings of a few great reformers, and it is true that much that is valuable in our present educational system can be understood and appreciated only when viewed in the perspective of such sources. Aristotle and Quintilian, Abelard and St. Thomas Aquinas, Sturm and Philip Melanchthon, Comenius, Pestalozzi, Rousseau, Herbart, and Froebel still live in the schools of to-day. Their genius speaks to us through the organization of subject-matter, through the art of questioning, through the developmental methods of teaching, through the use of pictures, through objective instruction, and in a thousand other forms. But this dominant ideal of education to which I have referred and which is so rapidly transforming our outlook and vitalizing our organization and inspiring us to new efforts, is not to be drawn from these sources. The new histories of education must account for this new ideal, and to do this they must turn to the masters in science who made the middle part of the nineteenth century the period of the most profound changes that the history of human thought records.[4]

With the illuminating principle of evolution came a new and generously rich conception of human growth and development. The panorama of evolution carried man back far beyond the limits of recorded human history and indicated an origin as lowly as the succeeding uplift has been sublime. The old depressing and fatalistic notion that the human race was on the downward path, and that the march of civilization must sooner or later end in a cul-de-sac (a view which found frequent expression in the French writers of the eighteenth century and which dominated the skepticism of the dark hours preceding the Revolution)—this fatalistic view met its death-blow in the principle of evolution. A vista of hope entirely undreamed of stretched out before the race. If the tremendous leverage of the untold millenniums of brute and savage ancestry could be overcome, even in slight measure, by a few short centuries of intelligence and reason, what might not happen in a few more centuries of constantly increasing light? In short, the principle of evolution supplied the perspective that was necessary to an adequate evaluation of human progress.

But this inspiriting outlook which was perhaps the most comprehensive result of Darwin's work had indirect consequences that were vitally significant to education. It is with mental and not with physical development that education is primarily concerned, and yet mental development is now known to depend fundamentally upon physical forces. The same decade that witnessed the publication of the *Origin of Species* also witnessed the birth of another great book, little known except to the specialist, and yet destined to achieve immortality. This book is the *Elements of Psychophysics*, the work of the German scientist Fechner. The intimate relation between mental life and physical and physiological forces was here first clearly demonstrated, and the way was open for a science of psychology which should cast aside the old and threadbare raiment of mystery and speculation and metaphysic, and stand forth naked and unashamed.

But all this was only preparatory to the epoch-making discoveries that have had so much to do with our present attitude toward education. The Darwinian hypothesis led to violent controversy, not only between the opponents and sup-

---

[4] While the years from 1840 to 1870 mark the period of intellectual revolution, it should not be inferred that the education of this period reflected these fundamental changes of outlook. On the contrary, these years were in general marked by educational stagnation.

porters of the theory, but also among the various camps of the evolutionists themselves. Among these controversies was that which concerned itself with the inheritance of acquired characteristics, and the outcome of that conflict has a direct significance to present educational theory. The principle, now almost conclusively established,[5] that the characteristics acquired by an organism during its lifetime are not transmitted by physical heredity to its offspring, must certainly stand as the basic principle of education; for everything that we identify as human as contrasted with that which is brutal must look to education for its preservation and support. It has been stated by competent authorities that, during the past ten thousand years, there has been no significant change in man's physical constitution. This simply means that Nature finished her work as far as man is concerned far beyond the remotest period that human history records; that, for all that we can say to-day, there must have existed in the very distant past human beings who were just as well adapted by nature to the lives that we are leading as we are to-day adapted; that what they lacked and what we possess is simply a mass of traditions, of habits, of ideals, and prejudices which have been slowly accumulated through the ages and which are passed on from generation to generation by imitation and instruction and training and discipline; and that the child of to-day, left to his own devices and operated upon in no way by the products of civilization, would develop into a savage undistinguishable in all significant qualities from other savages.

The possibilities that follow from such a conception are almost overwhelming even at first glance, and yet the theory is borne out by adequate experiments. The transformation of the Japanese people through two generations of education in Western civilization is a complete upsetting of the old theory that as far as race is concerned, there is anything significantly important in blood, and confirms the view that all that is racially significant depends upon the influences that surround the young of the race during the formative years. The complete assimilation of foreign ingredients into our own national stock through the instrumentality of the public school is another demonstration that the factors which form the significant characteristics in the lower animals possess but a minimum of significance to man,—that color, race, stature, and even brain weight and the shape of the cranium, have very little to do with human worth or human efficiency save in extremely abnormal cases.

And so we have at last a fundamental principle with which to illumine the field of our work and from which to derive not only light but inspiration. Unite this with John Fiske's penetrating induction that the possibilities of progress through education are correlated directly with the length of the period of growth or immaturity,—that is, that the races having the longest growth before maturity are capable of the highest degree of civilization,—and we have a pair of principles the influence of which we see reflected all about us in the great activity for education and especially in the increased sense of pride and responsibility and respect for his calling that is animating the modern teacher.

And what will be the result of this new point of view? First and foremost, an

[5] The writer here accepts the conclusions of J.A. Thomson (*Heredity* New York, 1908, ch. vii).

increased general respect for the work. Until a profession respects itself, it cannot very well ask for the world's respect, and until it can respect itself on the basis of scientific principles indubitably established, its respect for itself will be little more than the irritating self-esteem of the goody-goody order which is so often associated with our craft.

With our own respect for our calling, based upon this incontrovertible principle, will come, sooner or later, increased compensation for the work and increased prestige in the community. I repeat that these things can only come after we have established a true craft spirit. If we are ashamed of our calling, if we regret openly and publicly that we are not lawyers or physicians or dentists or bricklayers or farmers or anything rather than teachers, the public will have little respect for the teacher's calling. As long as we criticize each other before laymen and make light of each other's honest efforts, the public will question our professional standing on the ground that we have no organized code of professional ethics,—a prerequisite for any profession.

I started out to tell you something that we ought to be thankful for,—something that ought to counteract in a measure the inevitable tendencies toward pessimism and discouragement. The hopeful thing about our present status is that we have an established principle upon which to work. A writer in a recent periodical stoutly maintained that education was in the position just now that medicine was in during the Middle Ages. The statement is hardly fair, either to medicine or to education. If one were to attempt a parallel, one might say that education stands to-day where medicine stood about the middle of the nineteenth century. The analogy might be more closely drawn by comparing our present conception of education with the conception of medicine just prior to the application of the experimental method to a solution of its problems. Education has still a long road to travel before it reaches the point of development that medicine has to-day attained. It has still to develop principles that are comparable to the doctrine of lymph therapy or to that latest triumph of investigation in the field of medicine,—the theory of opsonins,—which almost makes one believe that in a few years violent accident and old age will be the only sources of death in the human race.

Education, we admit, has a long road to travel before it reaches so advanced a point of development. But there is no immediate cause for pessimism or despair. We need especially, now that the purpose of education is adequately defined, an adequate doctrine of educational values and a rich and vital infusion of the spirit of experimental science. For efficiency in the work of instruction and training, we need to know the influence of different types of experience in controlling human conduct,—we need to know just what degree of efficiency is exerted by our arithmetic and literature, our geography and history, our drawing and manual training, our Latin and Greek, our ethics and psychology. It is the lack of definite ideas and criteria in these fields that constitutes the greatest single source of waste in our educational system to-day.

And yet even here the outlook is extremely hopeful. The new movement toward industrial education is placing greater and greater emphasis upon those subjects of instruction and those types of methods whose efficiency can be tested and determined in an accurate fashion. The intimate relation between the classroom, on the one hand, and the machine shop, the experimental farm, the hospital ward and operating room, and the practice school, on the other hand, indicates a source of accurate knowledge with regard to the way in which our teachings really affect the conduct and adjustment of our pupils that cannot fail within a short time to serve as the basis for some illuminating principle of educational values. This, I believe, will be the next great step in the development of our profession.

There has been no intention in what I have said to minimize the disadvantages and discouragements under which we are to-day doing our work. My only plea is for the hopeful and optimistic outlook which, I maintain, is richly justified by the progress that has already been made and by the virile character of the forces that are operating in the present situation.

On the whole, I can see no reason why I should not encourage young men to enter the service of schoolcraft. I cannot say to them that they will attain to great wealth, but I can safely promise them that, if they give to the work of preparation the same attention and time that they would give to their education and training for medicine or law or engineering, their services will be in large demand and their rewards not to be sneered at. Their incomes will not enable them to compete with the captains of industry, but they will permit as full an enjoyment of the comforts of life as it is good for any young man to command. But the ambitious teacher must pay the price to reap these rewards,—the price of time and energy and labor,—the price that he would have to pay for success in any other human calling. What I cannot promise him in education is the opportunity for wide popular adulation, but this, after all, is a matter of taste. Some men crave it and they should go into those vocations that will give it to them. Others are better satisfied with the discriminating recognition and praise of their own fellow-craftsmen.

CHAPTER III

HOW MAY WE PROMOTE THE EFFICIENCY OF THE TEACHING FORCE?[6]

I

Efficiency seems to be a word to conjure with in these days. Popular speech has taken it in its present connotation from the technical vocabulary of engineering, and the term has brought with it a very refreshing sense of accuracy and practicality. It suggests blueprints and T-squares and mathematical formulæ. A faint and rather pleasant odor of lubricating oil and cotton waste seems to hover about it. The efficiency of a steam engine or a dynamo is a definitely determinable and measurable factor, and when we use the term "efficiency" in popular speech we convey through the word somewhat of this quality of certainty and exactitude.

An efficient man, very obviously, is a man who "makes good," who surmounts obstacles, overcomes difficulties, and "gets results." Rowan, the man who achieved immortality on account of a certain message that he carried to Garcia, is the contemporary standard of human efficiency. He was given a task to do, and he did it. He did not stop to inquire whether it was interesting, or whether it was easy, or whether it would be remunerative, or whether Garcia was a pleasant man to meet. He simply took the message and brought back the answer. Here we have efficiency in human endeavor reduced to its lowest terms: to take a message and to bring back an answer; to do the work that is laid out for one to do without shirking or "soldiering" or whining; and to "make good," to get results.

Now if we are to improve the efficiency of the teacher, the first thing to do is to see that the conditions of efficiency are fulfilled as far as possible at the outset. In other words, efficiency is impossible unless one is set a certain task to accomplish. Rowan was told to carry a message to Garcia. He was to carry it to Garcia, not to Queen Victoria or Li Hung Chang or J. Pierpont Morgan, or any one else whom he may have felt inclined to choose as its recipient. And that is just where Rowan had a decided advantage over many teachers who have every ambition to be just as efficient as he was. To expect a young teacher not only to get results, but also to determine the results that should be obtained, multiplies his chances of failure, not by two, as one might assume at first thought, but almost by infinity.

Let me give an example of what I mean. A young man graduated from college during the hard times of the middle nineties. It was imperative that he secure

[6] A paper read before the Normal and Training Teachers' Conference of the New York State Teachers' Association, December 27, 1907.

some sort of a remunerative employment, but places were very scarce and he had to seek a long time before he found anything to which he could turn his hand. The position that he finally secured was that of teacher in an ungraded school in a remote settlement. School-teaching was far from his thoughts and still farther from his ambitions, but forty dollars a month looked too good to be true, especially as he had come to the point where his allowance of food consisted of one plate of soup each day, with the small supply of crackers that went with it. He accepted the position most gratefully.

He taught this school for two years. He had no supervision. He read various books on the science and art of teaching and upon a certain subject that went by the name of psychology, but he could see no connection between what these books told him and the tasks that he had to face. Finally he bought a book that was advertised as indispensable to young teachers. The first words of the opening paragraph were these: "Teacher, if you know it all, don't read this book." The young man threw the volume in the fire. He had no desire to profit by the teaching of an author who began his instruction with an insult. From that time until he left the school, he never opened a book on educational theory.

His first year passed off with what appeared to be the most encouraging success. He talked to his pupils on science and literature and history. They were very good children, and they listened attentively. When he tired of talking, he set the pupils to writing in their copy books, while he thought of more things to talk about. He covered a great deal of ground that first year. Scarcely a field of human knowledge was left untouched. His pupils were duly informed about the plants and rocks and trees, about the planets and constellations, about atoms and molecules and the laws of motion, about digestion and respiration and the wonders of the nervous system, about Shakespeare and Dickens and George Eliot. And his pupils were very much interested in it all. Their faces had that glow of interest, that look of wonderment and absorption, that you get sometimes when you tell a little four-year-old the story of the three bears. He never had any troubles of discipline, because he never asked his pupils to do anything that they did not wish to do. There were six pupils in his "chart class." They were anxious to learn to read, and three of them did learn. Their mothers taught them at home. The other three were still learning at the end of the second year. He concluded that they had been "born short," but he liked them and they liked him. He did not teach his pupils spelling or writing. If they learned these things they learned them without his aid, and it is safe to say that they did not learn them in any significant measure. He did not like arithmetic, and so he just touched on it now and then for the sake of appearances.

This teacher was elected for the following year at a handsome increase of salary. He took this to mean a hearty indorsement of his methods; consequently he followed the same general plan the next year. He had told his pupils about everything that he knew, so he started over again, much to their delight. He left at the close of the year, amidst general lamentation. School-teaching was a delightful occupation, but he had mastered the art, and now he wished to attack something that was really difficult. He would study law. It is no part of the story that he did not. Neither is it part of the story that his successor had a very hard time getting that school straightened out; in fact, I believe it required three or four successive successors to make even an impression.

Now that man's work was a failure, and the saddest kind of a failure, for he did not realize that he had failed until years afterward. He failed, not because he lacked ambition and enthusiasm; he had a large measure of both these indispensable qualities. He failed, not because he lacked education and a certain measure of what the world calls culture; from the standpoint of education, he was better qualified than most teachers in schools of that type. He failed, not because he lacked social spirit and the ability to coöperate with the church and the home; he mingled with the other members of the community, lived their life and thought their thoughts and enjoyed their social diversions. The community liked him and respected him. His pupils liked him and respected him; and yet what he fears most of all to-day is that he may come suddenly face to face with one of those pupils and be forced to listen to a first-hand account of his sins of omission.

This man failed simply because he did not do what the elementary teacher must do if he is to be efficient as an elementary teacher. He did not train his pupils in the habits that are essential to one who is to live the social life. He gave them a miscellaneous lot of interesting information which held their attention while it lasted, but which was never mastered in any real sense of the term, and which could have but the most superficial influence upon their future conduct. But, worst of all, he permitted bad and inadequate habits to be developed at the most critical and plastic period of life. His pupils had followed the lines of least effort, just as he had followed the lines of least effort. The result was a well-established prejudice against everything that was not superficially attractive and intrinsically interesting.

Now this man's teaching fell short simply because he did not know what results he ought to obtain. He had been given a message to deliver, but he did not know to whom he should deliver it. Consequently he brought the answer, not from Garcia, but from a host of other personages with whom he was better acquainted, whose language he could speak and understand, and from whom he was certain of a warm welcome. In other words, having no definite results for which he would be held responsible, he did the kind of teaching that he liked to do. That might, under certain conditions, have been the best kind of teaching for his pupils. But these conditions did not happen to operate at that time. The answer that he brought did not happen to be the answer that was needed. That it pleased his employers does not in the least mitigate the failure. That a teacher pleases the community in which he works is not always evidence of his success. It is dangerous to make a statement like this, for some are sure to jump to the opposite conclusion and assume that one who is unpopular in the community is the most successful. Needless to say, the reasoning is fallacious. The matter of popularity is a secondary criterion, not a primary criterion of the efficiency of teaching. One may be successful and popular or successful and unpopular; unsuccessful and popular or unsuccessful and unpopular. The question of popularity is beside the question of efficiency, although it may enter into specific cases as a factor.

II

And so the first step to take in getting more efficient work from young teachers, and especially from inexperienced and untrained teachers fresh from the high school or the college, is to make sure that they know what is expected of them. Now this looks to be a very simple precaution that no one would be unwise enough to omit. As a matter of fact, a great many superintendents and principals are not explicit and definite about the results that they desire. Very frequently all that is asked of a teacher is that he or she keep things running smoothly, keep pupils and parents good-natured. Let me assert again that this ought to be done, but that it is no measure of a teacher's efficiency, simply because it can be done and often is done by means that defeat the purpose of the school. As a young principal in a city system, I learned some vital lessons in supervision from a very skillful teacher. She would come to me week after week with this statement: "Tell me what you want done, and I will do it." It took me some time to realize that that was just what I was being paid to do,—telling teachers what should be accomplished and then seeing that they accomplished the task that was set. When I finally awoke to my duties, I found myself utterly at a loss to make prescriptions. I then learned that there was a certain document known as the course of study, which mapped out the general line of work and indicated the minimal requirements. I had seen this course of study, but its function had never impressed itself upon me. I had thought that it was one of those documents that officials publish as a matter of form but which no one is ever expected to read. But I soon discovered that a principal had something to do besides passing from room to room, looking wisely at the work going on, and patting little boys and girls on the head.

Now a definite course of study is very hard to construct,—a course that will tell explicitly what the pupils of each grade should acquire each term or half-term in the way of habits, knowledge, ideals, attitudes, and prejudices. But such a course of study is the first requisite to efficiency in teaching. The system that goes by hit or miss, letting each teacher work out his own salvation in any way that he may see fit, is just an aggregation of such schools as that which I have described.

It is true that reformers have very strenuously criticized the policy of restricting teachers to a definite course of study. They have maintained that it curtails individual initiative and crushes enthusiasm. It does this in a certain measure. Every prescription is in a sense a restriction. The fact that the steamship captain must head his ship for Liverpool instead of wherever he may choose to go is a restriction, and the captain's individuality is doubtless crushed and his initiative limited. But this result seems to be inevitable and he generally manages to survive the blow. The course of study must be to the teacher what the sailing orders are to the captain of the ship, what the stated course is to the wheelsman and the officer on the bridge, what the time-table is to the locomotive engineer, what Garcia and the message and the answer were to Rowan. One may decry organization and prescription in our educational system. One may say that these things tend inevitably toward mechanism and formalism and the stultifying of initiative. But the fact remains that, whenever prescription is abandoned, efficiency in general is at an end.

And so I maintain that every teacher has a right to know what he is to be held responsible for, what is expected of him, and that this information be just as definite and unequivocal as it can be made. It is under the stress of definite responsibility that growth is most rapid and certain. The more uncertain and intangible the end to be gained, the less keenly will one feel the responsibility for gaining that end. Unhappily we cannot say to a teacher: "Here is a message. Take it to Garcia. Bring the answer." But we may make our work far more definite and tangible than it is now. The courses of study are becoming more and more explicit each year. Vague and general prescriptions are giving place to definite and specific prescriptions. The teachers know what they are expected to do, and knowing this, they have some measure for testing the efficiency of their own efforts.

III

But to make more definite requirements is, after all, only the first step in improving efficiency. It is not sufficient that one know what results are wanted; one must also know how these results may be obtained. Improvement in method means improvement in efficiency, and a crying need in education to-day is a scientific investigation of methods of teaching. Teachers should be made acquainted with the methods that are most economical and efficient. As a matter of fact, whatever is done in that direction at the present time must be almost entirely confined to suggestions and hints.

Our discussions of methods of teaching may be divided into three classes: (1) Dogmatic assertions that such and such a method is right and that all others are wrong—assertions based entirely upon *a priori* reasoning. For example, the assertion that children must never be permitted to learn their lessons "by heart" is based upon the general principle that words are only symbols of ideas and that, if one has ideas, one can find words of his own in which to formulate them. (2) A second class of discussions of method comprises descriptions of devices that have proved successful in certain instances and with certain teachers. (3) Of a third class of discussions there are very few representative examples. I refer to methods that have been established on the basis of experiments in which irrelevant factors have been eliminated. In fact, I know of no clearly defined report or discussion of this sort. An approach to a scientific solution of a definite problem of method is to be found in Browne's monograph, *The Psychology of Simple Arithmetical Processes.* Another example is represented by the experiments of Miss Steffens, Marx Lobsien, and others, regarding the best methods of memorizing, and proving beyond much doubt that the complete repetition is more economical than the partial repetition. But these conclusions have, of course, only a limited field of application to practical teaching. We stand in great need of a definite experimental investigation of the detailed problems of teaching upon which there is wide divergence of opinion. A very good illustration is the controversy between the how and the why in primary arithmetic. In this case, there is a vast amount of "opinion," but there are no clearly defined conclusions drawn from accurate tests. It would seem possible to do work of this sort concerning the details of method in the teaching of arithmetic, spelling, grammar, penmanship, and geography.

IV

Lacking this accurate type of data regarding methods, the next recourse is to the actual teaching of those teachers who are recognized as efficient. Wherever such a teacher may be found, his or her work is well worth the most careful sort of study. Success, of course, may be due to other factors than the methods employed,—to personality, for example. But, in every case of recognized efficiency in teaching that I have observed, I have found that the methods employed have, in the main, been productive of good results when used by others. The experienced teacher comes, through a process of trial and error, to select, perhaps unconsciously, the methods that work best. Sometimes these are not always to be identified with the methods that theoretical pedagogy had worked out from *a priori* bases. For example, the type of lesson which I call the "deductive development" lesson[7] is one that is not included in the older discussions of method; yet it accurately describes one of the methods employed by a very successful teacher whose work I observed.

One way, then, to improve the efficiency of young teachers, in so far as improvement in methods leads to improved efficiency, is to encourage the observation of expert teaching. The plan of giving teachers visiting days often brings excellent results, especially if the teacher looks upon the privilege in the proper light. The hyper-critical spirit is fatal to growth under any condition. Whenever a teacher has come to the conclusion that he or she has nothing to learn from studying the work of others, anabolism has ceased and katabolism has set in. The self-sufficiency of our craft is one of its weakest characteristics. It is the factor that more than any other discounts it in the minds of laymen. Fortunately it is less frequently a professional characteristic than in former years, but it still persists in some quarters. I recently met a "pedagogue" who impressed me as the most "knowing" individual that it had ever been my privilege to become acquainted with. An enthusiastic friend of his, in dilating upon this man's virtues, used these words: "When you propose a subject of conversation in whatever field you may choose, you will find that he has mastered it to bed rock. He will go over it once and you think that he is wise. He starts at the beginning and goes over it again, and you realize that he is deep. Once more he traverses the same ground, but he is so far down now that you cannot follow him, and then you are aware that he is profound." That sort of profundity is still not rare in the field of general education. The person who has all possible knowledge pigeonholed and classified is still in our midst. The pedant still does the cause of education incalculable injury.

Of the use to which reading circles may be put in improving the efficiency of teaching, it is necessary to say but little. Such organizations, under wise leadership, may doubtless be made to serve a good purpose in promoting professional enthusiasm. The difficulty with using them to promote immediate and direct efficiency lies in the paucity of the literature that is at our disposal. Most of our present-day works upon education are very general in their nature. They are not without their value, but this value is general and indirect rather than immediate and specific. A

[7] See *Educative Process*, New York, 1910, Chapter XX.

book like Miss Winterburn's *Methods of Teaching,* or Chubb's *Teaching of English*[8] is especially valuable for young teachers who are looking for first-hand helps. But books like this are all too rare in our literature.

On the whole, I think that the improvement of teachers in the matter of methods is the most unsatisfactory part of our problem.[9] All that one can say is that the work of the best teachers should be observed carefully and faithfully, that the methods upon which there is little or no dispute should be given and accepted as standard, but that one should be very careful about giving young teachers an idea that there is any single form under which all teaching can be subsumed. I know of no term that is more thoroughly a misnomer in our technical vocabulary than the term "general method." I teach a subject that often goes by that name, but I always take care to explain that the name does not mean, in my class, what the words seem to signify. There are certain broad and general principles which describe very crudely and roughly and inadequately certain phases of certain processes that mind undergoes in organizing experience—perception, apperception, conception, induction, deduction, inference, generalization, and the like. But these terms have only a vague and general connotation; or, if their connotation is specific and definite, it has been made so by an artificial process of definition in which counsel is darkened by words without meaning. The only full-fledged law that I know of in the educative process is the law of habit building—(1) focalization, (2) attentive repetition at intervals of increasing length, (3) permitting no exception—and I am often told that this "law" is fallacious. It has differed from some other so-called laws, however, in this respect: it always works. Whenever a complex habit is adduced that has not been formed through the operation of this law, I am willing to give it up.

V

A third general method of improving the efficiency of teaching is to build up the notion of responsibility for results. The teacher must not only take the message and deliver it to Garcia, or to some other individual as definite and tangible, but he must also bring the answer. So far as I know there is no other way to insure a maximum of efficiency than to demand certain results and to hold the individual responsible for gaining these results. The present standards of the teaching craft are less rigorous than they should be in this respect. We need a craft spirit that will judge every man impartially by his work, not by secondary criteria. You remem-

---

[8] Rowe's *Habit Formation* (New York, 1909), Briggs and Coffman's *Reading in Public Schools* (Chicago, 1908), Foght's *The American Rural School,* Adams's *Exposition and Illustration in Class Teaching* (New York, 1910), and Perry's *Problems of Elementary Education* (New York, 1910) should certainly be added to this list.

[9] "It seems to me one of the most pressing problems in pedagogy to-day is that of method. . . . It is the subject in which teachers of pedagogy in Colleges and Universities are weakest to-day. Of what practical value is all our study of educational psychology or the history of education, our child study, our experimental pedagogy, if it does not finally result in the devising of better methods of teaching, and make the teacher more skillful and effective in his work."—T.M. Balliet: "Undergraduate Instruction in Pedagogy," *Pedagogical Seminary,* vol. xvii, 1910, p. 67.

ber Finlayson in Kipling's *Bridge Builders*, and the agony with which he watched the waters of the Ganges tearing away at the caissons of his new bridge. A vital question of Finlayson's life was to be answered by the success or failure of those caissons to resist the flood. If they should yield, it meant not only the wreck of the bridge, but the wreck of his career; for, as Kipling says, "Government might listen, perhaps, but his own kind would judge him by his bridge as that stood or fell."

President Hall has said that one of the last sentiments to be developed in human nature is "the sense of responsibility, which is one of the highest and most complex psychic qualities." How to develop this sentiment of responsibility is one of the most pressing problems of education. And the problem is especially pressing in those departments of education that train for social service. To engender in the young teacher an effective prejudice against scamped work, against the making of excuses, against the seductive allurements of ease and comfort and the lines of least resistance is one of the most important duties that is laid upon the normal school, the training school, and the teachers' college. To do well the work that has been set for him to do should be the highest ambition of every worker, the ambition to which all other ambitions and desires are secondary and subordinate. Pride in the mastery of the technique of one's calling is the most wholesome and helpful sort of pride that a man can indulge in. The joy of doing each day's work in the best possible manner is the keenest joy of life. But this pride and this joy do not come at the outset. Like all other good things of life, they come only as the result of effort and struggle and strenuous self-discipline and dogged perseverance. The emotional coloring which gives these things their subjective worth is a matter very largely of contrast. Success must stand out against a background of struggle, or the chief virtue of success—the consciousness of conquest—will be entirely missed. That sort of success means strength; for strength of mind is nothing more than the ability to "hew to the line," to follow a given course of effort to a successful conclusion, no matter how long and how tedious be the road that one must travel, no matter how disagreeable are the tasks involved, no matter how tempting are the insidious siren songs of momentary fancy.

What teachers need—what all workers need—is to be inspired with those ideals and prejudices that will enable them to work steadfastly and unremittingly toward the attainment of a stated end. What inspired Rowan with those ideals of efficiency that enabled him to carry his message and bring back the answer, I do not know, but if he was a soldier, I do not hesitate to hazard an opinion. Our regular army stands as the clearest type of efficient service which is available for our study and emulation. The work of Colonel Goethals on the Panama Canal bids fair to be the finest fruit of the training that we give to the officers of our army. If we wish to learn the fundamental virtues of that training, it is not sufficient to study the curriculum of the Military Academy. Technical knowledge and skill are essential to such results, but they are not the prime essentials. If you wish to know what the prime essentials are, let me refer you to a series of papers, entitled *The Spirit of Old West Point*, which ran through a recent volume of the *Atlantic Monthly* and which has since been published in book form. They constitute, to my mind, one of the most important educational documents of the present decade. The army service is efficient because it is inspired with effective ideals of service,—ideals in which every other desire and ambition is totally and completely subordinated to the ideal of duty. To those who maintain that close organization and definite prescription kill initiative and curtail efficiency, the record of West Point and the army service should be a silencing argument.

And yet education is more important than war; more important, even, than the building of the Panama Canal. We believe, and rightly, that no training is too good for our military and naval officers; that no discipline which will produce the appropriate habits and ideals and prejudices is too strenuous; that no individual sacrifice of comfort or ease is too costly. Equal or even commensurable efficiency in education can come only through a like process. From the times of the ancient Egyptians to the present day, one vital truth has been revealed in every forward movement; the homely truth that you cannot make bricks without straw; you cannot win success without effort; you cannot attain efficiency without undergoing the processes of discipline; and discipline means only this: doing things that you do not want to do, for the sake of reaching some end that ought to be attained.

The normal schools and the training schools and the teachers' colleges must be the nurseries of craft ideals and standards. The instruction that they offer must be upon a plane that will command respect. The intolerable pedantry and the hypocritical goody-goodyism must be banished forever. The crass sentimentalism by which we attempt to cover our paucity of craft ideals must also be eliminated. Those who are most strongly imbued with ideals are not those who cheapen the value of ideals by constant verbal reiteration. Ideals do not often come through explicitly imparted precepts. They come through more impalpable and hidden channels,—now through stately buildings with vine-covered towers from which the past speaks in the silence of great halls and cloistered retreats; now through the unwritten and scarcely spoken traditions that are expressed in the very bearing and attitude of those to whom youth looks for inspiration and guidance; now through a dominant and powerful personality, sometimes rough and crude, sometimes warm-hearted and lovable, but always sincere. Traditions and ideals are the most priceless part of a school's equipment, and the school that can give these things to its students in richest measure will have the greatest influence on the succeeding generations.

CHAPTER IV

THE TEST OF EFFICIENCY IN SUPERVISION[10]

I

I know of no way in which I can better introduce my subject than to describe very briefly the work of a superintendent who once furnished me with an example of a definite and effective method of supervision. This man was a "long range" superintendent. It was impossible for him to visit his schools very frequently, and so he did the next best thing: he had the schools brought to him. When I first saw him he was poring over a pile of papers that had just come in from one of his schools. I soon discovered that these papers were arranged in sets, each set being made up of samples taken each week from the work of the pupils in the schools under his supervision. The papers of each pupil were arranged in chronological order, and by looking through the set, he could note the growth that the pupil in question had made since the beginning of the term. Upon these papers, the superintendent recorded his judgment of the amount of improvement shown both in form and in content.

I was particularly impressed by the character of his criticisms. There was nothing vague or intangible about them. Every annotation was clear and definite. If penmanship happened to be the point at issue, he would note that the lines were too close together; that the letters did not have sufficient individuality; that the spaces between the words were not sufficiently wide; that the indentation was inadequate; that the writing was cramped, showing that the pen had not been held properly; that the margin needed correction. If the papers were defective from the standpoint of language, the criticisms were equally clear and definite. One pupil had misspelled the same word in three successive papers. "Be sure that this word appears in the next spelling list," was the comment of the superintendent. Another pupil habitually used a bit of false syntax: "Place this upon the list of errors to be taken up and corrected." Still others were uncertain about paragraphing: "Devote a language lesson to the paragraph before the next written exercise." On the covers of each bundle of class papers, he wrote directions and suggestions of a more general nature; for example: "Improvement is not sufficiently marked; try for better results next time"; or: "I note that the pupils draw rather than write; look out for free movement." Often, too, there were words of well-merited praise: "I like the way in which your pupils have responded to their drill. This is good. Keep it up." And not infrequently suggestions were made as to content: "Tell this story

[10] A paper read before the fifty-second annual meeting of the New York State Association of School Commissioners and Superintendents, November 8, 1907.

in greater detail next time, and have it reproduced again"; or: "The form of these papers is good, but the nature study is poor; don't sacrifice thought to form."

In similar fashion, the other written work was gone over and annotated. Every pupil in this system of schools had a sample of his written work examined at regular and frequent intervals by the superintendent. Every teacher knew just what her chief demanded in the way of results, and did her best to gain the results demanded. I am not taking the position that the results that were demanded represented the highest ideals of what the elementary school should accomplish. Good penmanship and good spelling and good language, in the light of contemporary educational thought, seem to be something like happiness—you get them in larger measure the less you think about getting them. But this possible objection aside, the superintendent in question had developed a system which kept him in very close touch with the work that was being done in widely separated schools.

He told me further that, on the infrequent occasions when he could visit his classrooms, he gave most of his time and attention to the matters that could not be supervised at "long range." He found out how the pupils were improving in their reading, and especially in oral expression, in its syntax, its freedom from errors of construction, its clearness and fluency. He listed the common errors, directing his teachers to take them up in a systematic manner and eradicate them, and he did not fail to note at his next visit how much progress had been made. He noted the condition of the blackboard work, and kept a list of the improvements that he suggested. He tested for rapidity in arithmetical processes, for the papers sent to his office gave him only an index of accuracy. He noted the habits of personal cleanliness that were being developed or neglected. In fact, he had a long list of specific standards that he kept continually in mind, the progress toward which he constantly watched. And last, but by no means least, he carried with him wherever he went an atmosphere of breezy good nature and cheerfulness, for he had mastered the first principle in the art of both supervision and teaching; he had learned that the best way to promote growth in either pupils or teachers is neither to let them do as they please nor to force them to do as you please, but to get them to please to do what you please to have them do.

I instance this superintendent as one type of efficiency in supervision. He was efficient, not simply because he had a system that scrutinized every least detail of his pupils' growth, but because that scrutiny really insured growth. He obtained the results that he desired, and he obtained uniformly good results from a large number of young, untrained teachers. We have all heard of the superintendent who boasted that he could tell by looking at his watch just what any pupil in any classroom was doing at just that moment. Surely here system was not lacking. But the boast did not strike the vital point. It is not what the pupil is doing that is fundamentally important, but what he is gaining from his activity or inactivity; what he is gaining in the way of habits, in the way of knowledge, in the way of standards and ideals and prejudices, all of which are to govern his future conduct. The superintendent whom I have described had the qualities of balance and perspective that enabled him to see both the woods and the trees. And let me add that he taught regularly in his own central high school, and that practically all of his supervision was accomplished after school hours and on Saturdays.

But my chief reason for choosing his work as a type is that it represents a successful effort to supervise that part of school work which is most difficult and irksome to supervise; namely, the formation of habits. Whatever one's ideals of education may be, it still remains true that habit building is the most important duty of the elementary school, and that the efficiency of habit building can be tested in no other way than by the means that he employed; namely, the careful comparison of results at successive stages of the process.

II

The essence of a true habit is its purely automatic character. Reaction must follow upon the stimulus instantaneously, without thought, reflection, or judgment. One has not taught spelling efficiently until spelling is automatic, until the correct form flows from the pen without the intervention of mind. The real test of the pupil's training in spelling is his ability to spell the word correctly when he is thinking, not about spelling, but about the content of the sentence that he is writing. Consequently the test of efficiency in spelling is not an examination in spelling, although this may be valuable as a means to an end, but rather the infrequency with which misspelled words appear in the composition work, letter writing, and other written work of the pupil. Similarly in language and grammar, it is not sufficient to instruct in rules of syntax. This is but the initial process. Grammatical rules function effectively only when they function automatically. So long as one must think and judge and reflect upon the form of one's expression, the expression is necessarily awkward and inadequate.

The same rule holds in respect of the fundamental processes of arithmetic. It holds in penmanship, in articulation and enunciation, in word recognition, in moral conduct and good manners; in fact, in all of the basic work for which the elementary school must stand sponsor. And one source of danger in the newer methods of education lies in the tendency to overlook the importance of carrying habit-building processes through to a successful issue. The reaction against drill, against formal work of all sorts, is a healthful reaction in many ways. It bids fair to break up the mechanical lock step of the elementary grades, and to introduce some welcome life, and vigor, and wholesomeness. But it will sadly defeat its own purpose if it underrates the necessity of habit building as the basic activity of early education.

What is needed, now that we have got away from the lock step, now that we are happily emancipated from the meaningless thralldom of mechanical repetition and the worship of drill for its own sake—what is needed now is not less drill, but better drill. And this should be the net result of the recent reforms in elementary education. In our first enthusiasm, we threw away the spelling book, poked fun at the multiplication tables, decried basal reading, and relieved ourselves of much wit and sarcasm at the expense of formal grammar. But now we are swinging back to the adequate recognition of the true purpose of drill. And in the wake of this newer conception, we are learning that its drudgery may be lightened and its efficiency heightened by the introduction of a richer content that shall provide a greater variety in the repetitions, insure an adequate motive for effort, and relieve the dead monotony that frequently rendered the older methods so futile. I look forward to the time when to be an efficient drillmaster in this newer sense of the term will be to have reached one of the pinnacles of professional skill.

III

But there is another side of teaching that must be supervised. Although habit is responsible for nine tenths of conduct, the remaining tenth must not be neglected. In situations where habit is not adequate to adjustment, judgment and reflection must come to the rescue, or should come to the rescue. This means that, instead of acting without thought, as in the case of habit, one analyzes the situation and tries to solve it by the application of some fact or principle that has been gained either from one's own experience or from the experience of others. This is the field in which knowledge comes to its own; and a very important task of education is to fix in the pupils' minds a number of facts and principles that will be available for application to the situations of later life.

How, then, is the efficiency of instruction (as distinguished from training or habit building) to be tested? Needless to say, an adequate test is impossible from the very nature of the situation. The efficiency of imparting knowledge can be tested only by the effect that this knowledge has upon later conduct; and this, it will be agreed, cannot be accurately determined until the pupil has left the school and is face to face with the problems of real life.

In practice, however, we adopt a more or less effective substitute for the real test—the substitute called the examination. We all know that the ultimate purpose of instruction is not primarily to enable pupils successfully to pass examinations. And yet as long as we teach as though this were the main purpose we might as well believe it to be. Now the examination may be made a very valuable test of the efficiency of instruction if its limitations are fully recognized and if it does not obscure the true purpose of instruction. And if we remember that the true purpose is to impart facts in such a manner that they may not only "stick" in the pupil's mind, but that they may also be amenable to recall and practical application, and if we set our examination questions with some reference to this requirement, then I believe that we shall find the examination a dependable test.

One important point is likely to be overlooked in the consideration of examinations,—the fact, namely, that the form and content of the questions have a very powerful influence in determining the content and methods of instruction. Is it not pertinent, then, to inquire whether examination questions cannot be so framed as radically to improve instruction rather than to encourage, as is often the case, methods that are pedagogically unsound? Granted that it is well for the child to memorize verbatim certain unrelated facts, even to memorize some facts that have no immediate bearing upon his life, granted that this is valuable (and I think that a little of it is), is it necessary that an entire year or half-year be given over almost entirely to "cramming up" on old questions? Would it not be possible so to frame examination questions that the "cramming" process would be practically valueless?

What the pupil should get from geography, for instance, is not only a knowledge of geographical facts, but also, and more fundamentally, the power to see the relation of these facts to his own life; in other words, the ability to apply his knowledge to the improvement of adjustment. Now this power is very closely associated with the ability to grasp fundamental principles, to see the relation of cause and effect working below the surface of diverse phenomena. Geography, to be practical, must impress not only the fact, but also the principle that rationalizes or explains the fact. It must emphasize the "why" as well as the "what." For example: it is well for the pupil to know that New York is the largest city in the United States; it is better that he should know why New York has become the largest city in the United States. It is well to know that South America extends very much farther to the east than does North America, but it is better to know that this fact has had an important bearing in determining the commercial relations that exist between South America and Europe. Questions that have reference to these larger relations of cause and effect may be so framed that no amount of "cramming" will alone insure correct answers. They may be so framed that the pupil will be forced to do some thinking for himself, will be forced to solve an imaginary situation very much as he would solve a real situation.

Examination questions of this type would react beneficially upon the methods of instruction. They would tend to place a premium upon that type of instruction that develops initiative in solving problems, instead of encouraging the memoriter methods that tend to crush whatever germs of initiative the pupil may possess. This does not mean that the memoriter work should be excluded. A solid basis of fact is essential to the mastery of principles. Personally I believe that the work of the intermediate grades should be planned to give the pupil this factual basis. This would leave the upper grades free for the more rational work. In any case, I believe that the efficiency of examinations may be greatly increased by giving one or two questions that must be answered by a reasoning process for every question that may be answered by verbal memory alone.

IV

Thus far it seems clear that an absolute standard is available for testing the efficiency of training or habit building, and that a fairly accurate standard may be developed for testing the efficiency of instruction. Both training and instruction, however, are subject to the modifying influence of a third factor of which too little account has hitherto been taken in educational discussions. Training results in habits, and yet a certain sort of training may not only result in a certain type of habit, but it may also result in the development of something which will quite negate the habit that has been developed. In the process of developing habits of neatness, for example, one may employ methods that result in prejudicing the child against neatness as a general virtue. In this event, although the little specific habits of neatness may function in the situations in which they have been developed, the prejudice will effectually prevent their extension to other fields. In other words, the general emotional effect of training must be considered as well as the specific results of the training. The same stricture applies with equal force to instruction. Instruction imparts knowledge; but if a man knows and fails to feel, his knowledge has little influence upon his conduct.

This factor that controls conduct when habit fails, this factor that may even negate an otherwise efficient habit, is the great indeterminate in the work of teaching. To know that one has trained an effective habit or imparted a practical principle is one thing; to know that in doing this, one has not engendered in the pupil's mind a prejudice against the very thing taught is quite another matter.

That phase of teaching which is concerned with the development of these intangible forces may be termed "inspiration"; and it is the lack of an adequate test for the efficiency of inspiration that makes the task of supervision so difficult and the results so often unsatisfactory.

Nevertheless, even here the outlook is not entirely hopeless. One may be tolerably certain of at least two things. In the first place, the great "emotionalized prejudices" that must come predominantly from school influences are the love of truth, the love of work, respect for law and order, and a spirit of coöperation. These factors undoubtedly have their basis in specific habits of honesty, industry, obedience, and regard for the rights and feelings of others; and these habits may be developed and tested just as thoroughly and just as accurately as habits of good spelling and correct syntax. Without the solid basis of habit, ideals and prejudices will be of but little service. The one caution must be taken that the methods of training do not defeat their own purpose by engendering prejudices and ideals that negate the habits. It is here that the personality of the teacher becomes the all-important factor, and the task of the supervisor is to determine whether the influence of the personality is good or evil. Most supervisors come to judge of this influence by an undefined factor that is best termed the "spirit of the classroom."

The second hopeful feature of the task of supervision in respect of inspiration is that this "spirit" is an extremely contagious and pervasive thing. In other words, the principal or the superintendent may dominate every classroom under his supervision, almost without regard to the limitations of the individual teachers. Typical schools in every city system bear compelling testimony to this fact. The principal *is* the school.

And if I were to sum up the essential characteristics of the ideal supervisor, I could not neglect this point. After all, the two great dangers that beset him are, first, the danger of sloth—the old Adam of laziness—which will tempt him to avoid the details, to shirk the drudgery, to escape the close and wearisome scrutiny of little things; and, secondly, the sin of triviality—the inertia which holds him to details and never permits him to take the broader view and see the true ends toward which details are but the means. The proper combination of these two factors is all too rare, but it is in this combination that the ideal supervisor is to be found.

CHAPTER V

THE SUPERVISOR AND THE TEACHER

I

It is difficult not to be depressed by the irrational radicalism of contemporary educational theory. It would seem that the workers in the higher ranges of educational activity should, of all men, preserve a balanced judgment and a sane outlook, and yet there is probably no other human calling that presents the strange phenomenon of men who are called experts throwing overboard everything that the past has sanctioned, and embarking without chart or compass upon any new venture that happens to catch popular fancy. The non-professional character of education is nowhere more painfully apparent than in the expression of this tendency. The literature of teaching that is written directly out of experience—out of actual adjustment to the teaching situation—is almost laughed out of court in some educational circles. But if one wishes to win the applause of the multitude one may do it easily enough by proclaiming some new and untried plan. At our educational gatherings you notice above everything else a straining for spectacular and bizarre effects. It is the novel that catches attention; and it sometimes seems to me that those who know the least about the educational situation in the way of direct contact often receive the largest share of attention and have the largest influence.

It is in the attitude of the public and of a certain proportion of school men toward elementary teaching and the elementary teacher that this destructive criticism finds its most pronounced expression. Throughout the length and breadth of the land, the efficiency of the public school and the sincerity and intelligence of those who are giving their lives to its work are being called into question. It is discouraging to think that years of service in a calling do not qualify one to speak authoritatively upon the problems of that calling, and especially upon technique. And yet it is precisely upon that point of technique that the criticisms of elementary education are most drastic.

Our educational system is sometimes branded as a failure, and yet this same educational system with all its weaknesses has accomplished the task of assimilating to American institutions and ideals and standards the most heterogeneous infusion of alien stocks that ever went to the making of a united people. The elementary teacher is criticized for all the sins of omission that the calendar enumerates, and yet this same elementary teacher is daily lifting millions of children to a plane of civilization and culture that no other people in history have even thought possible. I am willing to admit the deficiencies of American education, but I also maintain that the teachers of our lower schools do not deserve the opprobrium that has been heaped upon them. I believe that in education, as in business, it would be a good thing if we saw more of the doughnut and less of the hole. When I hear a prominent educator say that we must discard everything that we have produced thus far and begin anew in the realm of educational materials and methods, I confess that I am discouraged, especially when that same authority is extremely obscure as to the materials and methods that we should substitute for those that we are now employing. I heard that statement at a recent meeting of the Department of Superintendence, and I heard other things of like tenor,—for example, that normal schools were perpetuating types of skill in teaching that were unworthy of perpetuation, that the observation of teaching was valueless in the training of teachers because there was nothing that was being done at the present time that was worthy of imitation, that practice teaching in the training of young teachers is a farce, a delusion, and a snare. Those very words were employed by one man of high position to express his opinion of contemporary practices. You cannot pick up an educational journal of the better sort, nor open a new educational book, without being brought face to face with this destructive criticism.

I protest against this, not only in the name of justice, but in the name of common sense. It cannot be possible that generations of dealing with immature minds should have left no residuum of effective practice. The very principle of progress by trial and error will inevitably mean that certain practices that are possible and helpful and effective are perpetuated, and that certain other processes that are ineffective and wasteful are eliminated. To repudiate all this is the height of folly. If the history of progress shows us anything, it shows us that progress is not made by repudiating the lessons of experience. Theory is the last word, not the first. Theory should explain: it should take successful practice and find out what principles condition its efficiency; and if these principles are inconsistent with those heretofore held, it is the theory that should be modified to suit the facts, not the facts to suit the theory.

My opponents may point to medicine as a possible example of the opposite procedure. And yet if there is anything that the history of medical science demonstrates, it is that the first cues to new discoveries were made in the field of practice. Lymph therapy, which is one of the triumphs of modern medicine, was discovered empirically. It was an accident of practice, a blind procedure of trial and success that led to Jenner's discovery of the virtues of vaccination. A century passed before theory adequately explained the phenomenon, and opened the way to those wider applications of the principle that have done so much to reduce the ravages of disease.

The value of theory, I repeat, is to explain successful practice and to generalize experience in broad and comprehensive principles which can be easily held in mind, and from which inferences for further new and effective practices may be derived. We have a small body of sound principles in education to-day,—a body of principles that are thoroughly consistent with successful practice. But the sort of principles that are put forth as the last words of educational theory are often far from sound. Personally I firmly believe that a vast amount of damage is being done to children by the application of fallacious principles which, because they emanate from high authority, obtain an artificial validity in the minds of teachers in service.

I cannot understand why, when an educational experiment fails lamentably, it is not rejected as a failure. And yet you and I know a number of instances where certain educational experiments that have undeniably reversed the hypotheses of those who initiated them are excused on the ground that conditions were not favorable. That, it seems to me, should tell the whole story, for precisely what we need in educational practice is a body of doctrine that will work where conditions *are* unfavorable. We are told that the successful application of mooted theories depends upon the proper kind of teachers. I maintain that the most effective sort of theory is the sort that brings results with such teachers as we must employ in our work. It would be a poor recommendation for a theory of medicine to say that it worked all right when people are healthy but failed to help the sick. Nor is it true that good teachers can get good results by following bad theory. They often obtain the results by evading the theory, and when they live up to it, the results faithfully reflect the theory, no matter how skillful the teaching.

II

Statements like these are very apt to be misconstrued or misinterpreted unless one is very careful to define one's position; and, after what I have said, I should do myself an injustice if I did not make certain that my position is clear. I believe in experimentation in education. I believe in experimental schools. But I should wish these schools to be interpreted as experiments and not as models, and I should wish that the failure of an experiment be accepted with good, scientific grace, and not with the unscientific attitude of making excuses. The trouble with an experimental school is that, in the eyes of the great mass of teachers, it becomes a model school, and the principles that it represents are applied *ad libitum* by thousands of teachers who assume that they have heard the last word in educational theory.

No one is more favorably disposed toward the rights of children than I am, and yet I am thoroughly convinced that soft-heartedness accompanied by soft-headedness is weakening the mental and moral fiber of hundreds of thousands of boys and girls throughout this country. No one admires more than I admire the sagacity and far-sightedness of Judge Lindsey, and yet when Judge Lindsey's methods are proposed as models for school government, I cannot lose sight, as so many people seem to lose sight, of the contingent factor; namely, that Judge Lindsey's leniency is based upon authority, and that if Judge Lindsey or anybody else attempted to be lenient when he had no power to be otherwise than lenient, his "bluff" would be called in short order. If you will give to teachers and principals the same power that you give to the police judge, you may well expect them to be lenient. The great trouble in the school is simply this: that just in the proportion that leniency is demanded, authority is taken away from the teacher.

And I should perhaps say a qualifying word with regard to my attitude toward educational theory. I have every feeling of affection for the science of psychology. I have every faith in the value of psychological principles in the interpretation of educational phenomena. But I also recognize that the science of psychology is a very young science, and that its data are not yet so well organized that it is safe to draw from them anything more than tentative hypotheses which must meet their final test in the crucible of practice. Some day, if we work hard enough, psychology will become a predictive science, just as mathematics and physics and chemistry and, to a certain extent, biology, are predictive sciences to-day. Meantime psychology is of inestimable value in giving us a point of view, in clarifying our ideas, and in rationalizing the truths that empirical practice discovers. A very few psychological principles are strongly enough established even now to form the basis of prediction. Among the most important of these are the laws of habit building, some laws of memory, and the larger principles of attention. Successful educational practice is and must be in accord with these indisputable tenets. But the bane of education to-day is in the pseudo-science, the "half-baked" psychology, that is lauded from the house-tops by untrained enthusiasts, turned from the presses by irresponsible publishing houses, and foisted upon the hungry teaching public through the ever-present medium of the reading circle, the teachers' institute, the summer school, and I am very sorry to admit (for I think that I represent both institutions in a way) sometimes by the normal schools and universities.

Most of the doctrines that are turning our practice topsy-turvy have absolutely no support from competent psychologists. The doctrine of spontaneity and its attendant *laissez-faire* dogma of school government is thoroughly inconsistent with good psychology. The radical extreme to which some educators would push the doctrine of interest when they maintain that the child should never be asked to do anything for which he fails to find a need in his own life,—this doctrine can find no support in good psychology. The doctrine that the preadolescent child should understand thoroughly every process that he is expected to reduce to habit before that process is made automatic is utterly at variance with long-established principles which were well understood by the Greeks and the Hebrews twenty-five hundred years ago, and to which Mother Nature herself gives the lie in the instincts of imitation and repetition. It is conceivable that these radical doctrines were justified as means of reform, especially in secondary and higher education, but, even granting this, their function is fulfilled when the reform that they exploited has been accomplished. That time has come and, as palpable untruths, they should either be modified to meet the facts, or be relegated to oblivion.

III

It is safe to say that formalism is no longer a characteristic feature of the typical American school. It is so long since I have heard any rote learning in a schoolroom that I am wondering if it is not almost time for some one to show that a little rote learning would not be at all a bad thing in preadolescent education. We ridicule the memoriter methods of Chinese education and yet we sometimes forget that Chinese education has done something that no other system of education, however well planned, has even begun to do in the same degree. It has kept the Chinese empire a unit through a period of time compared with which the entire history of Greece and Rome is but an episode. We may ridicule the formalism of Hebrew education, and yet the schools of rabbis have preserved intact the racial integrity of the Jewish people during the two thousand years that have elapsed since their geographical unity was destroyed. I am not justifying the methods of Chinese or Hebrew education. I am quite willing to admit that, in China at any rate, the game may not have been worth the candle; but I am still far from convinced that it is not a good thing for children to reduce to verbal form a good many things that are now never learned in such a way as to make any lasting impression upon the memory; and our criticism of oriental formalism is not so much concerned with the method of learning as with the content of learning,—not so much with learning by heart as with the character of the material that was thus memorized.

But, although formalism is no longer a distinctive feature of American education, formalism is the point from which education is most frequently attacked,—and this is the chief source of my dissatisfaction with the present-day critics of our elementary schools. In a great many cases, they have set up a man of straw and demolished him completely. And in demolishing him, they have incidentally knocked the props from under the feet of many a good teacher, leaving him dazed and uncertain of his bearings, stung with the conviction that what he has been doing for his pupils is entirely without value, that his life of service has been a failure, that the lessons of his own experience are not to be trusted, nor the verdicts of his own intelligence respected. Go to any of the great summer schools and you will meet, among the attending teachers, hundreds of faithful, conscientious men and women who could tell you if they would (and some of them will) of the muddle in which their minds are left after some of the lectures to which they have listened. Why should they fail to be depressed? The whole weight of academic authority seems to be against them. The entire machinery of educational administration is wheeling them with relentless force into paths that seem to them hopelessly intricate and bewildering. If it is true, as I think it is, that some of the proposals of modern education are an attempt to square the circle, it is certainly true that the classroom teacher is standing at the pressure points in this procedure.

We hear expressed on every side a great deal of sympathy for the child as the victim of our educational system. Sympathy for childhood is the most natural thing in the world. It is one of the basic human instincts, and its expressions are among the finest things in human life. But why limit our sympathy to the child, especially to-day when he is about as happy and as fortunate an individual as anybody has ever been in all history. Why not let a little of it go out to the teacher of this child? Why not plan a little for her comfort and welfare and encouragement? It is her skill that is assimilating the children of our alien population. It is her strength that is lifting bodily each generation to the ever-advancing race levels. Her work must be the main source of the inspiration that will impel the race to further advancement. And yet when these half-million teachers who mean so much to this country gather at their institutes, when they attend the summer schools, when they take up their professional journals, what do they hear and read? Criticisms of their work. Denunciations of their methods. Serious doubts of their intelligence. Aspersions cast upon their sincerity, their patience, and their loyalty to their superiors. This, mingled with some mawkish sentimentalism that passes under the name of inspiration. Only occasionally a word of downright commendation, a sign of honest and heartfelt appreciation, a note of sympathy or encouragement.

Carnegie gives fifteen million dollars to provide pensions for superannuated college professors; but the elementary teacher who is not fortunate enough to die in harness must look forward to the almshouse. The people tax themselves for magnificent buildings and luxurious furnishings, but not one cent do they offer for teachers' pensions. What a blot upon Western civilization is this treatment of the teachers in our lower schools. These people are doing the work that even the savage races universally consider to be of the highest type. Benighted China places her teachers second only to the literati themselves in the place of honor. The Hindus made the teaching profession the highest caste in the social scale. The Jews intrusted the education of their children to their Rabbis, the most learned and the most honored of their race. It is only Western civilization—it is almost only our much-lauded Anglo-Saxon civilization—that denies to the teacher a station in life befitting his importance as a social servant.

IV

But what has all this to do with school supervision? As I view it, the supervisor of schools as the overseer and director of the educational process, is just now confronted with two great problems. The first of these is to keep a clear head in the present muddled condition of educational theory. From the very fact of his position, the supervisor must be a leader, whether he will or not. It is a maxim of our profession that the principal is the school. In our city systems the supervising principal is given almost absolute authority over the school of which he has charge. In him is vested the ultimate responsibility for instruction, for discipline, for the care and condition of the material property. He may be a despot if he wishes, benevolent or otherwise. With this power goes a corresponding opportunity. His school can stand for something,—perhaps for something new and strange which will bring him into the limelight to-day, no matter what its character; perhaps for something solid and enduring, something that will last long after his own name has been forgotten. The temptation was never so strong as it is to-day for the supervisor to seek the former kind of glory. The need was never more acute than it is to-day for the supervisor who is content with the impersonal glory of the latter type.

I admit that it is a somewhat thankless task to do things in a straightforward, effective way, without fuss or feathers, and I suppose that the applause of the gallery may be easily mistaken for the applause of the pit. But nevertheless the seeker for notoriety is doing the cause of education a vast amount of harm. I know a principal who won ephemeral fame by introducing into his school a form of the Japanese jiu-jitsu physical exercises. When I visited that school, I was led to believe that jiu-jitsu would be the salvation of the American people. Whole classes of girls and boys were marched to the large basement to be put through their paces for the delectation of visitors. The newspapers took it up and heralded it as another indication that the formalism of the public school was gradually breaking down.

Visitors came by the hundreds, and my friend basked in the limelight of public adulation while his colleagues turned green with envy and set themselves to devising some means for turning attention in their direction.

And yet, there are some principals who move on in the even tenor of their ways, year after year, while all these currents and countercurrents are seething and eddying around them. They hold fast to that which they know is good until that which they know is better can be found. They believe in the things that they do, so the chances are greatly increased that they will do them well. They refuse to be bullied or sneered at or laughed out of court because they do not take up with every fancy that catches the popular mind. They have their own professional standards as to what constitutes competent schoolmanship,—their own standards gained from their own specialized experience. And somehow I cannot help thinking that just now that is the type of supervisor that we need and the type that ought to be encouraged. If I were talking to Chinese teachers, I might preach another sort of gospel, but American education to-day needs less turmoil, less distraction, fewer sweeping changes. It needs to settle itself, and look around, and find out where it is and what it is trying to do. And it needs, above all, to rise to a consciousness of itself as an institution manned by intelligent individuals who are perfectly competent themselves to set up craft standard and ideals.

V

But in whatever way the supervisor may utilize the opportunity that his position presents, his second great problem will come up for solution. The supervisor is the captain of the teaching corps. Directly under his control are the mainsprings of the school's life and activity,—the classroom teachers. It is coming to be a maxim in the city systems that the supervisor has not only the power to mold the school to the form of his own ideals, but that he can, if he is skillful, turn weak teachers into strong teachers and make out of most unpromising material, an efficient, homogeneous school staff. I believe that this is coming to be considered the prime criterion of effective school supervision,—not what skill the supervisor may show in testing results, or in keeping his pupils up to a given standard, or in choosing his teachers skillfully, but rather the success with which he is able to take the teaching material that is at his hand, and train it into efficiency.

A former Commissioner of Education for one of our new insular possessions once told me that he had come to divide supervisors into two classes,—(1) those who knew good teaching when they saw it, and (2) those who could make poor teachers into good teachers. Of these two types, he said, the latter were infinitely more valuable to pioneer work in education than the former, and he named two or three city systems from which he had selected the supervisors who could do this sort of thing,—for there is no limit to this process of training, and the superintendent who can train supervisors is just as important as the supervisor who can train teachers.

It would take a volume adequately to treat the various problems that this conception of the supervisor's function involves. I can do no more at present than indicate what seems to me the most pressing present need in this direction. I have found that sometimes the supervisors who insist most strenuously that their teachers secure the coöperation of their pupils are among the very last to secure for themselves the coöperation of their teachers.

And to this important end, it seems to me that we have an important suggestion in the present condition of the classroom teacher as I have attempted to describe it. As a type, the classroom teacher needs just now some adequate appreciation and recognition of the work that she is doing. If the lay public is unable adequately to judge the teacher's work, there is all the more reason that she should look to her supervisor for that recognition of technical skill, for that commendation of good work, which can come only from a fellow-craftsman, but which, when it does come, is worth more in the way of real inspiration than the loudest applause of the crowd.

Upon the whole, I believe that the outlook in this direction is encouraging. While the teacher may miss in her institutes and in the summer school that sort of encouragement, she is, I believe, finding it in larger and larger measure in the local teachers' meetings and in her consultations with her supervisors. And when all has been said, that is the place from which she should look for inspiration. The teachers' meeting must be the nursery of professional ideals. It must be a place where the real first-hand workers in education get that sanity of outlook, that professional point of view, which shall fortify them effectively against the rising tide of unprofessional interference and dictation which, as I have tried to indicate, constitutes the most serious menace to our educational welfare.

And it is in the encouragement of this craft spirit, in this lifting of the teacher's calling to the plane of craft consciousness, it is in this that the supervisor must, I believe, find the true and lasting reward for his work. It is through this factor that he can, just now, work the greatest good for the schools that he supervises and the community that he serves. The most effective way to reach his pupils is through the medium of their teachers, and he can help these pupils in no better way than to give their teachers a justifiable pride in the work that they are doing through his own recognition of its worth and its value, through his own respect for the significance of the lessons that experience teaches them, through his own suggestive help in making that experience profitable and suggestive. And just at the present moment, he can make no better start than by assuring them of the truth that Emerson expresses when he defines the true scholar as the man who remains firm in his belief that a popgun is only a popgun although the ancient and honored of earth may solemnly affirm it to be the crack of doom.

CHAPTER VI

EDUCATION AND UTILITY[11]

I

I wish to discuss with you some phases of the problem that is perhaps foremost in the minds of the teaching public to-day: the problem, namely, of making education bear more directly and more effectively upon the work of practical, everyday life. I have no doubt that some of you feel, when this problem is suggested, very much as I felt when I first suggested to myself the possibility of discussing it with you. You have doubtless heard some phases of this problem discussed at every meeting of this association for the past ten years—if you have been a member so long as that. Certain it is that we all grow weary of the reiteration of even the best of truths, but certain it is also that some problems are always before us, and until they are solved satisfactorily they will always stimulate men to devise means for their solution.

I should say at the outset, however, that I shall not attempt to justify to this audience the introduction of vocational subjects into the elementary and secondary curriculums. I shall take it for granted that you have already made up your minds upon this matter. I shall not take your time in an attempt to persuade you that agriculture ought to be taught in the rural schools, or manual training and domestic science in all schools. I am personally convinced of the value of such work and I shall take it for granted that you are likewise convinced.

My task to-day, then, is of another type. I wish to discuss with you some of the implications of this matter of utility in respect of the work that every elementary school is doing and always must do, no matter how much hand work or vocational material it may introduce. My problem, in other words, concerns the ordinary subject-matter of the curriculum,—reading and writing and arithmetic, geography and grammar and history,—those things which, like the poor, are always with us, but which we seem a little ashamed to talk about in public. Truly, from reading the educational journals and hearing educational discussion to-day, the layman might well infer that what we term the "useful" education and the education that is now offered by the average school are as far apart as the two poles. We are all familiar with the statement that the elementary curriculum is eminently adapted to produce clerks and accountants, but very poorly adapted to furnish recruits for any other department of life. The high school is criticized on the ground that

[11] An address before the Eastern Illinois Teachers' Association, October 15, 1909. Published as a Bulletin of the Eastern Illinois Normal School, October, 1909.

it prepares for college and consequently for the professions, but that it is totally inadequate to the needs of the average citizen. Now it would be futile to deny that there is some truth in both these assertions, but I do not hesitate to affirm that both are grossly exaggerated, and that the curriculum of to-day, with all its imperfections, does not justify so sweeping a denunciation. I wish to point out some of the respects in which these charges are fallacious, and, in so doing, perhaps, to suggest some possible remedies for the defects that every one will acknowledge.

II

In the first place, let me make myself perfectly clear upon what I mean by the word "useful." What, after all, is the "useful" study in our schools? What do men find to be the useful thing in their lives? The most natural answer to this question is that the useful things are those that enable us to meet effectively the conditions of life,—or, to use a phrase that is perfectly clear to us all, the things that help us in getting a living. The vast majority of men and women in this world measure all values by this standard, for most of us are, to use the expressive slang of the day, "up against" this problem, and "up against" it so hard and so constantly that we interpret everything in the greatly foreshortened perspective of immediate necessity. Most of us in this room are confronting this problem of making a living. At any rate, I am confronting it, and consequently I may lay claim to some of the authority that comes from experience.

And since I have made this personal reference, may I violate the canons of good taste and make still another? I was face to face with this problem of getting a living a good many years ago, when the opportunity came to me to take a college course. I could see nothing ahead after that except another struggle with this same vital issue. So I decided to take a college course which would, in all probability, help me to solve the problem. Scientific agriculture was not developed in those days as it has been since that time, but a start had been made, and the various agricultural colleges were offering what seemed to be very practical courses. I had had some early experience on the farm, and I decided to become a scientific farmer. I took the course of four years and secured my degree. The course was as useful from the standpoint of practical agriculture as any that could have been devised at the time. But when I graduated, what did I find? The same old problem of getting a living still confronted me as I had expected that it would; and alas! I had got my education in a profession that demanded capital. I was a landless farmer. Times were hard and work of all kinds was very scarce. The farmers of those days were inclined to scoff at scientific agriculture. I could have worked for my board and a little more, and I should have done so had I been able to find a job. But while I was looking for the place, a chance came to teach school, and I took the opportunity as a means of keeping the wolf from the door. I have been engaged in the work of teaching ever since. When I was able to buy land, I did so, and I have to-day a farm of which I am very proud. It does not pay large dividends, but I keep it up for the fun I get out of it,—and I like to think, also, that if I should lose my job as a teacher, I could go back to the farm and show the natives how to make money. This is doubtless an illusion, but it is a source of solid comfort just the same.

Now the point of this experience is simply this: I secured an education that seemed to me to promise the acme of utility. In one way, it has fulfilled that promise far beyond my wildest expectations, but that way was very different from the one that I had anticipated. The technical knowledge that I gained during those four strenuous years, I apply now only as a means of recreation. So far as enabling me directly to get a living, this technical knowledge does not pay one per cent on the investment of time and money. And yet I count the training that I got from its mastery as, perhaps, the most useful product of my education.

Now what was the secret of its utility? As I analyze my experience, I find it summed up very largely in two factors. In the first place, I studied a set of subjects for which I had at the outset very little taste. In studying agriculture, I had to master a certain amount of chemistry, physics, botany, and zoölogy, for each and every one of which I felt, at the outset, a distinct aversion and dislike. A mastery of these subjects was essential to a realization of the purpose that I had in mind. I was sure that I should never like them, and yet, as I kept at work, I gradually found myself losing that initial distaste. First one and then another opened out its vista of truth and revelation before me, and almost before I was aware of it, I was enthusiastic over science. It was a long time before I generalized that experience and drew its lesson, but the lesson, once learned, has helped me more even in the specific task of getting a living than anything else that came out of my school training. That experience taught me, not only the necessity for doing disagreeable tasks,—for attacking them hopefully and cheerfully,—but it also taught me that disagreeable tasks, if attacked in the right way, and persisted in with patience, often become attractive in themselves. Over and over again in meeting the situations of real life, I have been confronted with tasks that were initially distasteful. Sometimes I have surrendered before them; but sometimes, too, that lesson has come back to me, and has inspired me to struggle on, and at no time has it disappointed me by the outcome. I repeat that there is no technical knowledge that I have gained that compares for a moment with that ideal of patience and persistence. When it comes to real, downright utility, measured by this inexorable standard of getting a living, let me commend to you the ideal of persistent effort. All the knowledge that we can learn or teach will come to very little if this element is lacking.

Now this is very far from saying that the pursuit of really useful knowledge may not give this ideal just as effectively as the pursuit of knowledge that will never be used. My point is simply this: that beyond the immediate utility of the facts that we teach,—indeed, basic and fundamental to this utility,—is the utility of the ideals and standards that are derived from our school work. Whatever we teach, these essential factors can be made to stand out in our work, and if our pupils acquire these we shall have done the basic and important thing in helping them to solve the problems of real life,—and if our pupils do not acquire these, it will make little difference how intrinsically valuable may be the content of our instruction. I feel like emphasizing this matter to-day, because there is in the air a notion that utility depends entirely upon the content of the curriculum. Certainly the curriculum must be improved from this standpoint, but we are just now losing sight of the other equally important factor,—that, after all, while both are essential, it is the spirit of teaching rather than the content of teaching that is basic and fundamental.

Nor have I much sympathy with that extreme view of this matter which asserts that we must go out of our way to provide distasteful tasks for the pupil in order to develop this ideal of persistence. I believe that such a policy will always tend to defeat its own purpose. I know a teacher who holds this belief. He goes out of his way to make tasks difficult. He refuses to help pupils over hard places. He does not believe in careful assignments of lessons, because, he maintains, the pupil ought to learn to overcome difficulties for himself, and how can he learn unless real difficulties are presented?

The great trouble with this teacher is that his policy does not work out in practice. A small minority of his pupils are strengthened by it; the majority are weakened. He is right when he says that a pupil gains strength only by overcoming difficulties, but he neglects a very important qualification of this rule, namely, that a pupil gains no strength out of obstacles that he fails to overcome. It is the conquest that comes after effort,—this is the factor that gives one strength and confidence. But when defeat follows defeat and failure follows failure, it is weakness that is being engendered—not strength. And that is the trouble with this teacher's pupils. The majority leave him with all confidence in their own ability shaken out of them and some of them never recover from the experience.

And so while I insist strenuously that the most useful lesson we can teach our pupils is how to do disagreeable tasks cheerfully and willingly, please do not understand me to mean that we should go out of our way to provide disagreeable tasks. After all, I rejoice that my own children are learning how to read and write and cipher much more easily, much more quickly, and withal much more pleasantly than I learned those useful arts. The more quickly they get to the plane that their elders have reached, the more quickly they can get beyond this plane and on to the next level.

To argue against improved methods in teaching on the ground that they make things too easy for the pupil is, to my mind, a grievous error. It is as fallacious as to argue that the introduction of machinery is a curse because it has diminished in some measure the necessity for human drudgery. But if machinery left mankind to rest upon its oars, if it discouraged further progress and further effortful achievement, it *would* be a curse: and if the easier and quicker methods of instruction simply bring my children to my own level and then fail to stimulate them to get beyond my level, then they are a curse and not a blessing.

I do not decry that educational policy of to-day which insists that school work should be made as simple and attractive as possible. I do decry that misinterpretation of this policy which looks at the matter from the other side, and asserts so vehemently that the child should never be asked or urged to do something that is not easy and attractive. It is only because there is so much in the world to be done that, for the sake of economizing time and strength, we should raise the child as quickly and as rapidly and as pleasantly as possible to the plane that the race has reached. But among all the lessons of race experience that we must teach him there is none so fundamental and important as the lesson of achievement itself,—the supreme lesson wrung from human experience,—the lesson, namely, that every advance that the world has made, every step that it has taken forward, every increment that has been added to the sum total of progress has been attained at the price of self-sacrifice and effort and struggle,—at the price of doing things that one does not want to do. And unless a man is willing to pay that price, he is bound to be the worst kind of a social parasite, for he is simply living on the experience of others, and adding to this capital nothing of his own.

It is sometimes said that universal education is essential in order that the great mass of humanity may live in greater comfort and enjoy the luxuries that in the past have been vouchsafed only to the few. Personally I think that this is all right so far as it goes, but it fails to reach an ultimate goal. Material comfort is justified only because it enables mankind to live more effectively on the lower planes of life and give greater strength and greater energy to the solution of new problems upon the higher planes of life. The end of life can never be adequately formulated in terms of comfort and ease, nor even in terms of culture and intellectual enjoyment; the end of life is achievement, and no matter how far we go, achievement is possible only to those who are willing to pay the price. When the race stops investing its capital of experience in further achievement, when it settles down to take life easily, it will not take it very long to eat up its capital and revert to the plane of the brute.

III

But I am getting away, from my text. You will remember that I said that the most useful thing that we can teach the child is to attack strenuously and resolutely any problem that confronts him whether it pleases him or not, and I wanted to be certain that you did not misinterpret me to mean that we should, for this reason, make our school tasks unnecessarily difficult and laborious. After all, while our attitude should always be one of interesting our pupils, their attitude should always be one of effortful attention,—of willingness to do the task that we think it best for them to do. You see it is a sort of a double-headed policy, and how to carry it out is a perplexing problem. Of so much I am certain, however, at the outset: if the pupil takes the attitude that we are there to interest and entertain him, we shall make a sorry fiasco of the whole matter, and inasmuch as this very tendency is in the air at the present time, I feel justified in at least referring to its danger.

Now if this ideal of persistent effort is the most useful thing that can come out of education, what is the next most useful? Again, as I analyze what I obtained from my own education, it seems to me that, next to learning that disagreeable tasks are often well worth doing, the factor that has helped me most in getting a living has been the method of solving the situations that confronted me. After all, if we simply have the ideal of resolute and aggressive and persistent attack, we may struggle indefinitely without much result. All problems of life involve certain common factors. The essential difference between the educated and the uneducated man, if we grant each an equal measure of pluck, persistence, and endurance, lies in the superior ability of the educated man to analyze his problem effectively and to proceed intelligently rather than blindly to its solution. I maintain that education should give a man this ideal of attacking any problem; furthermore I maintain that the education of the present day, in spite of the anathemas that are hurled against it, is doing this in richer measure than it has ever been done before. But there is no reason why we should not do it in still greater measure.

I once knew two men who were in the business of raising fruit for commercial purposes. Each had a large orchard which he operated according to conventional methods and which netted him a comfortable income. One of these men was a man of narrow education: the other a man of liberal education, although his training had not been directed in any way toward the problems of horticulture. The orchards had borne exceptionally well for several years, but one season, when the fruit looked especially promising, a period of wet, muggy weather came along just before the picking season, and one morning both these men went out into their orchards, to find the fruit very badly "specked." Now the conventional thing to do in such cases was well known to both men. Each had picked up a good deal of technical information about caring for fruit, and each did the same thing in meeting this situation. He got out his spraying outfit, prepared some Bordeaux mixture, and set vigorously at work with his pumps. So far as persistence and enterprise went, both men stood on an equal footing. But it happened that this was an unusual and not a conventional situation. The spraying did not alleviate the condition. The corruption spread through the trees like wildfire, and seemed to thrive on copper sulphate rather than succumb to its corrosive influence.

Now this was where the difference in training showed itself. The orchardist who worked by rule of thumb, when he found that his rule did not work, gave up the fight and spent his time sitting on his front porch bemoaning his luck. The other set diligently at work to analyze the situation. His education had not taught him anything about the characteristics of parasitic fungi, for parasitic fungi were not very well understood when he was in school. But his education had left with him a general method of procedure for just such cases, and that method he at once applied. It had taught him how to find the information that he needed, provided that such information was available. It had taught him that human experience is crystallized in books, and that, when a discovery is made in any field of science,—no matter how specialized the field and no matter how trivial the finding,—the discovery is recorded in printer's ink and placed at the disposal of those who have the intelligence to find it and apply it. And so he set out to read up on the subject,—to see what other men had learned about this peculiar kind of apple rot. He obtained all that had been written about it and began to master it. He told his friend about this material and suggested that the latter follow the same course, but the man of narrow education soon found himself utterly at sea in a maze of technical terms. The terms were new to the other too, but he took down his dictionary and worked them out. He knew how to use indices and tables of contents and various other devices that facilitate the gathering of information, and while his uneducated friend was storming over the pedantry of men who use big words, the other was making rapid progress through the material. In a short time he learned everything that had been found out about this specific disease. He learned that its spores are encased in a gelatinous sac which resisted the entrance of the chemicals.

He found how the spores were reproduced, how they wintered, how they germinated in the following season; and, although he did not save much of his crop that year, he did better the next. Nor were the evidences of his superiority limited to this very useful result. He found that, after all, very little was known about this disease, so he set himself to find out more about it. To do this, he started where other investigators had left off, and then he applied a principle he had learned from his education; namely, that the only valid methods of obtaining new truths are the methods of close observation and controlled experiment.

Now I maintain that the education which was given that man was effective in a degree that ought to make his experience an object lesson for us who teach. What he had found most useful at a very critical juncture of his business life was, primarily, not the technical knowledge that he had gained either in school or in actual experience. His superiority lay in the fact that he knew how to get hold of knowledge when he needed it, how to master it once he had obtained it, how to apply it once he had mastered it, and finally how to go about to discover facts that had been undetected by previous investigators. I care not whether he got this knowledge in the elementary school or in the high school or in the college. He might have secured it in any one of the three types of institution, but he had to learn it somewhere, and I shall go further and say that the average man has to learn it in some school and under an explicit and conscious method of instruction.

IV

But perhaps you would maintain that this statement of the case, while in general true, does not help us out in practice. After all, how are we to impress pupils with this ideal of persistence and with these ideals of getting and applying information, and with this ideal of investigation? I maintain that these important useful ideals may be effectively impressed almost from the very outset of school life. The teaching of every subject affords innumerable opportunities to force home their lessons. In fact, it must be a very gradual process—a process in which the concrete instances are numerous and rich and impressive. From these concrete instances, the general truth may in time emerge. Certainly the chances that it will emerge are greatly multiplied if we ourselves recognize its worth and importance, and lead our pupils to see in each concrete case the operation of the general principle. After all, the chief reason why so much of our education miscarries, why so few pupils gain the strength and the power that we expect all to gain, lies in the inability of the average individual to draw a general conclusion from concrete cases—to see the general in the particular. We have insisted so strenuously upon concrete instruction that we have perhaps failed also to insist that fact without law is blind, and that observation without induction is stupidity gone to seed.

Let me give a concrete instance of what I mean. Not long ago, I visited an eighth-grade class during a geography period. It was at the time when the discovery of the Pole had just set the whole civilized world by the ears, and the teacher was doing something that many good teachers do on occasions of this sort: she was turning the vivid interest of the moment to educative purposes. The pupils had read Peary's account of his trip and they were discussing its details in class.

Now that exercise was vastly more than an interesting information lesson, for Peary's achievement became, under the skillful touch of that teacher, a type of all human achievement. I wish that I could reproduce that lesson for you—how vividly she pictured the situation that confronted the explorer,—the bitter cold, the shifting ice, the treacherous open leads, the lack of game or other sources of food supply, the long marches on scant rations, the short hours and the uncomfortable conditions of sleep; and how from these that fundamental lesson of pluck and endurance and courage came forth naturally without preaching the moral or indulging in sentimental "goody-goodyism." And then the other and equally important part of the lesson,—how pluck and courage in themselves could never have solved the problem; how knowledge was essential, and how that knowledge had been gained: some of it from the experience of early explorers,—how to avoid the dreaded scurvy, how to build a ship that could withstand the tremendous pressure of the floes; and some from the Eskimos,—how to live in that barren region, and how to travel with dogs and sledges;—and some, too, from Peary's own early experiences,—how he had struggled for twenty years to reach the goal, and had added this experience to that until finally the prize was his. We may differ as to the value of Peary's deed, but that it stands as a type of what success in any undertaking means, no one can deny. And this was the lesson that these eighth-grade pupils were absorbing,—the world-old lesson before which all others fade into insignificance,—the lesson, namely, that achievement can be gained only by those who are willing to pay the price.

And I imagine that when that class is studying the continent of Africa in their geography work, they will learn something more than the names of rivers and mountains and boundaries and products,—I imagine that they will link these facts with the names and deeds of the men who gave them to the world. And when they study history, it will be vastly more than a bare recital of dates and events,—it will be alive with these great lessons of struggle and triumph,—for history, after all, is only the record of human achievement. And if those pupils do not find these same lessons coming out of their own little conquests,—if the problems of arithmetic do not furnish an opportunity to conquer the pressure ridges of partial payments or the Polar night of bank discount, or if the intricacies of formal grammar do not resolve themselves into the North Pole of correct expression,—I have misjudged that teacher's capacities; for the great triumph of teaching is to get our pupils to see the fundamental and the eternal in things that are seemingly trivial and transitory. We are fond of dividing school studies into the cultural and the practical, into the humanities and the sciences. Believe me, there is no study worth the teaching that is not practical at basis, and there is no practical study that has not its human interest and its humanizing influence—if only we go to some pains to search them out.

V

I have said that the most useful thing that education can do is to imbue the pupil with the ideal of effortful achievement which will lead him to do cheerfully and effectively the disagreeable tasks that fall to his lot. I have said that the next most useful thing that it can do is to give him a general method of solving the problems that he meets. Is there any other useful outcome of a general nature that we may rank in importance with these two? I believe that there is, and I can perhaps tell you what I mean by another reference to a concrete case. I know a man who lacks this third factor, although he possesses the other two in a very generous measure. He is full of ambition, persistence, and courage. He is master of the rational method of solving the problems that beset him. He does his work intelligently and effectively. And yet he has failed to make a good living. Why? Simply because of his standard of what constitutes a good living. Measured by my standard, he is doing excellently well. Measured by his own standard, he is a miserable failure. He is depressed and gloomy and out of harmony with the world, simply because he has no other standard for a good living than a financial one. He is by profession a civil engineer. His work is much more remunerative than is that of many other callings. He has it in him to attain to professional distinction in that work. But to this opportunity he is blind. In the great industrial center in which he works, he is constantly irritated by the evidences of wealth and luxury beyond what he himself enjoys. The millionaire captain of industry is his hero, and because he is not numbered among this class, he looks at the world through the bluest kind of spectacles.

Now, to my mind that man's education failed somewhere, and its failure lay in the fact that it did not develop in him ideals of success that would have made him immune to these irritating factors. We have often heard it said that education should rid the mind of the incubus of superstition, and one very important effect of universal education is that it does offer to all men an explanation of the phenomena that formerly weighted down the mind with fear and dread, and opened an easy ingress to the forces of superstition and fraud and error. Education has accomplished this function, I think, passably well with respect to the more obvious sources of superstition. Necromancy and magic, demonism and witchcraft, have long since been relegated to the limbo of exposed fraud. Their conquest has been one of the most significant advances that man has made above the savage. The truths of science have at last triumphed, and, as education has diffused these truths among the masses, the triumph has become almost universal.

But there are other forms of superstition besides those I have mentioned,—other instances of a false perspective, of distorted values, of inadequate standards. If belief in witchcraft or in magic is bad because it falls short of an adequate interpretation of nature,—if it is false because it is inconsistent with human experience,—then the worship of Mammon that my engineer friend represents is tenfold worse than witchcraft, measured by the same standards. If there is any lesson that human history teaches with compelling force, it is surely this: Every race which has yielded to the demon of individualism and the lust for gold and self-gratification has gone down the swift and certain road to national decay. Every race that, through unusual material prosperity, has lost its grip on the eternal verities of self-sacrifice and self-denial has left the lesson of its downfall written large upon the pages of history. I repeat that if superstition consists in believing something that is inconsistent with rational human experience, then our present worship of the golden calf is by far the most dangerous form of superstition that has ever befuddled the human intellect.

But, you ask, what can education do to alleviate a condition of this sort? How may the weak influence of the school make itself felt in an environment that has crystallized on every hand this unfortunate standard? Individualism is in the air. It is the dominant spirit of the times. It is reënforced upon every side by the unmistakable evidences of national prosperity. It is easy to preach the simple life, but who will live it unless he has to? It is easy to say that man should have social and not individual standards of success and achievement, but what effect will your puerile assertion have upon the situation that confronts us?

Yes; it is easier to be a pessimist than an optimist. It is far easier to lie back and let things run their course than it is to strike out into midstream and make what must be for the pioneer a fatal effort to stem the current. But is the situation absolutely hopeless? If the forces of education can lift the Japanese people from barbarism to enlightenment in two generations; if education can in a single century transform Germany from the weakest to the strongest power on the continent of Europe; if five short years of a certain type of education can change the course of destiny in China;—are we warranted in our assumption that we hold a weak weapon in this fight against Mammon?

I have intimated that the attitude of my engineer friend toward life is the result of twisted ideals. A good many young men are going out into life with a similar defect in their education. They gain their ideals, not from the great wellsprings of human experience as represented in history and literature, in religion and art, but from the environment around them, and consequently they become victims of this superstition from the outset. As a trainer of teachers, I hold it to be one important part of my duty to fortify my students as strongly as I can against this false standard of which my engineer friend is the victim. It is just as much a part of my duty to give my students effective and consistent standards of what a good living consists in as it is to give them the technical knowledge and skill that will enable them to make a good living. If my students who are to become teachers have standards of living and standards of success that are inconsistent with the great ideal of social service for which teaching stands, then I have fallen far short of success in my work. If they are constantly irritated by the evidences of luxury beyond their means, if this irritation sours their dispositions and checks their spontaneity, their efficiency as teachers is greatly lessened or perhaps entirely negated. And if my engineer friend places worldly emoluments upon a higher plane than professional efficiency, I dread for the safety of the bridges that he builds. His education as an engineer should have fortified him against just such a contingency. It should have left him with the ideal of craftsmanship supreme in his life. And if his technical education failed to do this, his general education ought, at least, to have given him a bias in the right direction.

I believe that all forms of vocational and professional education are not so strong in this respect as they should be. Again you say to me, What can education do when the spirit of the times speaks so strongly on the other side? But what is education for if it is not to preserve midst the chaos and confusion of troublous times the great truths that the race has wrung from its experience? How different might have been the fate of Rome, if Rome had possessed an educational system touching every child in the Empire, and if, during the years that witnessed her decay and downfall, those schools could have kept steadily, persistently at work, impressing upon every member of each successive generation the virtues that made the old Romans strong and virile—the virtues that enabled them to lay the foundations of an empire that crumbled in ruins once these truths were forgotten. Is it not the specific task of education to represent in each generation the human experiences that have been tried and tested and found to work,—to represent these in the face of opposition if need be,—to be faithful to the trusteeship of the most priceless legacy that the past has left to the present and to the future? If this is not our function in the scheme of things, then what is our function? Is it to stand with bated breath to catch the first whisper that will usher in the next change? Is it to surrender all initiative and simply allow ourselves to be tossed hither and yon by the waves and cross-waves of a fickle public opinion? Is it to cower in dread of a criticism that is not only unjust but often ill-advised of the real conditions under which we are doing our work?

I take it that none of us is ready to answer these questions in the affirmative. Deep down in our hearts we know that we have a useful work to do, and we know that we are doing it passably well. We also know our defects and shortcomings at least as well as one who has never faced our problems and tried to solve them. And it is from this latter type that most of the drastic criticism, especially of the elementary and secondary school, emanates. I confess that my gorge rises within me when I read or hear the invectives that are being hurled against teaching as a profession (and against the work of the elementary and secondary school in particular) by men who know nothing of this work at first hand. This is the greatest handicap under which the profession of teaching labors. In every other important field of human activity a man must present his credentials before he takes his seat at the council table, and even then he must sit and listen respectfully to his elders for a while before he ventures a criticism or even a suggestion. This plan may have its defects. It may keep things on too conservative a basis; but it avoids the danger into which we as a profession have fallen,—the danger of "half-baked" theories and unmatured policies. To-day the only man that can get a respectable hearing at our great national educational meetings is the man who has something new and bizarre to propose. And the more startling the proposal, the greater is the measure of adulation that he receives. The result of this is a continual straining for effect, an enormous annual crop of fads and fancies, which, though most of them are happily short-lived, keep us in a state of continual turmoil and confusion.

Now, it goes without saying that there are many ways of making education hit the mark of utility in addition to those that I have mentioned. The teachers down in the lower grades who are teaching little children the arts of reading and writing and computation are doing vastly more in a practical direction than they are ever given credit for doing; for reading and writing and the manipulation of numbers are, next to oral speech itself, the prime necessities in the social and industrial world. These arts are being taught to-day better than they have ever been taught before,—and the technique of their teaching is undergoing constant refinement and improvement.

The school can do and is doing other useful things. Some schools are training their pupils to be well mannered and courteous and considerate of the rights of others. They are teaching children one of the most basic and fundamental laws of human life; namely, that there are some things that a gentleman cannot do and some things that society will not stand. How many a painful experience in solving this very problem of getting a living could be avoided if one had only learned this lesson passing well! What a pity it is that some schools that stand to-day for what we call educational progress are failing in just this particular—are sending out into the world an annual crop of boys and girls who must learn the great lesson of self-control and a proper respect for the rights of others in the bitter school of experience,—a school in which the rod will never be spared, but whose chastening scourge comes sometimes, alas, too late!

There is no feature of school life which has not its almost infinite possibilities of utility. But after all, are not the basic and fundamental things these ideals that I have named? And should not we who teach stand for idealism in its widest sense? Should we not ourselves subscribe an undying fidelity to those great ideals for which teaching must stand,—to the ideal of social service which lies at the basis of our craft, to the ideals of effort and discipline that make a nation great and its children strong, to the ideal of science that dissipates the black night of ignorance and superstition, to the ideal of culture that humanizes mankind?

CHAPTER VII

THE SCIENTIFIC SPIRIT IN EDUCATION[12]

I

I know that I do not need to plead with this audience for a recognition of the scientific spirit in the solution of educational problems. The long life and the enviable record of this Society of Pedagogy testify in themselves to that spirit of free inquiry, to the calm and dispassionate search for the truth which lies at the basis of the scientific method. You have gathered here, fortnight after fortnight, to discuss educational problems in the light of your experience. You have reported your experience and listened to the results that others have gleaned in the course of their daily work. And experience is the corner stone of science.

Some of the most stimulating and clarifying discussions of educational problems that I have ever heard have been made in the sessions of this Society. You have been scientific in your attitude toward education, and I may add that I first learned the lessons of the real science of education in the St. Louis schools, and under the inspiration that was furnished by the men who were members of this Society. What I knew of the science of education before I came to this city ten years ago, was gleaned largely from books. It was deductive, *a priori*, in its nature. What I learned here was the induction from actual experience.

My very first introduction to my colleagues among the school men of this city was a lesson in the science of education. I had brought with me a letter to one of your principals. He was in the office down on Locust Street the first Saturday that I spent in the city. I presented my letter to him, and, with that true Southern hospitality which has always characterized your corps, he took me immediately under his wing and carried me out to luncheon with him.

We sat for hours in a little restaurant down on Sixth Street,—he was my teacher and I was his pupil. And gradually, as the afternoon wore on, I realized that I had met a master craftsman in the art of education. At first I talked glibly enough of what I intended to do, and he listened sympathetically and helpfully, with a little quizzical smile in his eyes as I outlined my ambitious plans. And when I had run the gamut of my dreams, he took his turn, and, in true Socratic fashion, yet without making me feel in the least that I was only a dreamer after all, he refashioned my theories. One by one the little card houses that I had built up were deftly, smoothly, gently, but completely demolished. I did not know the ABC of schoolcraft—but he did not tell me that I did not. He went at the task of instruction

[12] An address delivered before the St. Louis Society of Pedagogy, April 16, 1910.

from the positive point of view. He proved to me, by reminiscence and example, how different are actual and ideal conditions. And finally he wound up with a single question that opened a new world to me. "What," he asked, "is the dominant characteristic of the child's mind?" I thought at first that I was on safe ground—for had I not taken a course in child study, and had I not measured some hundreds of school children while working out a university thesis? So I began with my list. But, at each characteristic that I mentioned he shook his head. "No," he said, "no; that is not right." And when finally I had exhausted my list, he said to me, "The dominant characteristic of the child's mind is its *seriousness*. The child is the most *serious* creature in the world."

The answer staggered me for a moment. Like ninety-nine per cent of the adult population of this globe, the seriousness of the child had never appealed to me. In spite of the theoretical basis of my training, that single, dominant element of child life had escaped me. I had gained my notion of the child from books, and, I also fear, from the Sunday supplements. To me, deep down in my heart, the child was an animated joke. I was immersed in unscientific preconceptions. But the master craftsman had gained his conception of child life from intimate, empirical acquaintance with the genus boy. He had gleaned from his experience that fundamental truth: "The child is the most serious creature in the world."

Sometime I hope that I may make some fitting acknowledgment of the debt of gratitude that I owe to that man. The opportunities that I had to talk with him were all too few, but I did make a memorable visit to his school, and studied at first hand the great work that he was doing for the pupils of the Columbia district. He died the next year, and I shall never forget the words that stood beneath his picture that night in one of the daily papers: "Charles Howard: Architect of Character."

II

The essence of the scientific spirit is to view experience without prejudice, and that was the lesson that I learned from the school system of St. Louis.

The difference between the ideal child and the real child,—the difference between what fancy pictures a schoolroom to be and what actual first-hand acquaintance shows that it is, the difference between a preconceived notion and an actual stubborn fact of experience,—these were among the lessons that I learned in these schools. But, at the same time, there was no crass materialism accompanying this teaching. There was no loss of the broader point of view. A fact is a fact, and we cannot get around it,—and this is what scientific method has insisted upon from its inception. But always beyond the fact is its significance, its meaning. That the St. Louis schools have for the last fifty years stood for the larger view; that they have never, so far as I know, exploited the new and the bizarre simply because it was new and strange,—this is due, I believe, to the insight and inspiration of the man[13] who first fashioned the framework of this system, and breathed into it as a system the vitalizing element of idealism. Personally, I have not always been in sympathy with the teachings of the Hegelian philosophy,—I have not always understood them,—but no man could witness the silent, steady, unchecked

[13] Dr. W.T. Harris.

growth of the St. Louis schools without being firmly and indelibly impressed with dynamic value of a richly conceived and rigidly wrought system of fundamental principles. The cause of education has suffered much from the failure of educators to break loose from the shackles of the past. But it has, in some places, suffered still more from the tendency of the human mind to confuse fundamental principles with the shackles of tradition. The rage for the new and the untried, simply because it is new and untried,—this has been, and is to-day, the rock upon which real educational progress is most likely to be wrecked. This is a rock, I believe, that St. Louis has so far escaped, and I have no doubt that its escape has been due, in large measure, to the careful, rigid, laborious, and yet illuminating manner in which that great captain charted out its course.

III

Fundamentally, there is, I believe, no discrepancy, no inconsistency, between the scientific spirit in education and what may be called the philosophical spirit. As I have suggested, there are always two dangers that must be avoided: the danger, in the first place, of thinking of the old as essentially bad; and, on the other hand, the danger of thinking of the new and strange and unknown as essentially bad; the danger of confusing a sound conservatism with a blind worship of established custom; and the danger of confusing a sound radicalism with the blind worship of the new and the bizarre.

Let me give you an example of what I mean. There is a rather bitter controversy at present between two factions of science teachers. One faction insists that physics and chemistry and biology should be taught in the high school from the economic point of view,—that the economic applications of these sciences to great human arts, such as engineering and agriculture, should be emphasized at every point,—that a great deal of the material now taught in these sciences is both useless and unattractive to the average high-school pupil. The other faction maintains that such a course would mean the destruction of science as an integral part of the secondary culture course,—that science to be cultural must be pure science,—must be viewed apart from its economic applications,—apart from its relations to the bread-and-butter problem.

Now many of the advocates of the first point of view—many of the people that would emphasize the economic side—are animated by the spirit of change and unrest which dominates our latter-day civilization. They wish to follow the popular demand. "Down with scholasticism!" is their cry; "Down with this blind worship of custom and tradition! Let us do the thing that gives the greatest immediate benefit to our pupils. Let us discard the elements in our courses that are hard and dry and barren of practical results." Now these men, I believe, are basing their argument upon the fallacy of immediate expediency. The old is bad, the new is good. That is their argument. They have no sheet anchor out to windward. They are willing to drift with the gale.

Many of the advocates of the second point of view—many of the people who hold to the old line, pure-science teaching—are, on the other hand, animated by a spirit of irrational conservatism. "Down with radicalism!" they shout; "Down with the innovators! Things that are hard and dry are good mental discipline. They made our fathers strong. They can make our children strong. What was good enough for the great minds of the past is good enough for us."

Now these men, I believe, have gone to the other extreme. They have confused custom and tradition with fundamental and eternal principles. They have thought that, just because a thing is old, it is good, just as their antagonists have thought that just because a thing is new it is good.

In both cases, obviously, the scientific spirit is lacking. The most fundamental of all principles is the principle of truth. And yet these men who are teachers of science are—both classes of them—ruled themselves by dogma. And meantime the sciences are in danger of losing their place in secondary education. The rich promise that was held out a generation ago has not been fulfilled. Within the last decade, the enrollment in the science courses has not increased in proportion to the total enrollment, while the enrollment in Latin (which fifteen years ago was about to be cast upon the educational scrap heap) has grown by leaps and bounds.

Now this is a type of a great many controversies in education. We talk and theorize, but very seldom do we try to find out the actual facts in the case by any adequate tests.

It was the lack of such tests that led us at the University of Illinois to enter upon a series of impartial investigations to see whether we could not take some of these mooted questions out of the realm of eternal controversy, and provide some definite solutions. We chose among others this controversy between the economic scientists and the pure scientists. We took a high-school class and divided it into two sections. We tried to place in each section an equal number of bright and mediocre and dull pupils, so that the conditions would be equalized. Then we chose an excellent teacher, a man who could approach the problem with an open mind, without prejudice or favor. During the present year he has been teaching these parallel sections. In one section he has emphasized economic applications; in the other he has taught the class upon the customary pure-science basis. He has kept a careful record of his work, and at stated intervals he has given both sections the same tests. We propose to carry on this investigation year after year with different classes, different teachers, and in different schools. We are not in a hurry to reach conclusions.

Now I said that the safeguard in all work of this sort is to keep our grip firm and fast on the eternal truths. In this work that I mention we are not trying to prove that either pure science or applied science interests our pupils the more or helps them the more in meeting immediate economic situations. We do not propose to measure the success of either method by its effect upon the bread-winning power of the pupil. What we believe that science teaching should insure, is a grip on the scientific method and an illuminating insight into the forces of nature, and we are simply attempting to see whether the economic applications will make this grip firmer or weaker, and this insight clearer or more obscure. I trust that this point is plain, for it illustrates what I have just said regarding the danger of following a popular demand. We need no experiment to prove that economic science is more useful in the narrow sense than is pure science. What we wish to determine is whether a judicious mixture of the two sorts of teaching will or will not enable us to realize this rich cultural value much more effectively than a traditional purely cultural course.

Now that illustrates what I think is the real and important application of the scientific spirit to the solution of educational problems. You will readily see that it does not do away necessarily with our ideals. It is not necessarily materialistic. It is not necessarily idealistic. Either side may utilize it. It is a quite impersonal factor. But it does promise to take some of our educational problems out of the field of useless and wasteful controversy, and it does promise to get men of conflicting views together,—for, in the case that I have just cited, if we prove that the right admixture of methods may enable us to realize both a cultural and a utilitarian value, there is no reason why the culturists and the utilitarians should not get together, cease their quarreling, take off their coats, and go to work. Few people will deny that bread and butter is a rather essential thing in this life of ours; very few will deny that material prosperity in temperate amounts is good for all of us; and very few also will deny that far more fundamental than bread and butter—far more important than material prosperity—are the great fundamental and eternal truths which man has wrought out of his experience and which are most effectively crystallized in the creations of pure art, the masterpieces of pure literature, and the discoveries of pure science.

Certainly if we of the twentieth century can agree upon any one thing, it is this: That life without toil is a crime, and that any one who enjoys leisure and comfort and the luxuries of living without paying the price of toil is a social parasite. I believe that it is an important function of public education to impress upon each generation the highest ideals of living as well as the arts that are essential to the making of a livelihood, but I wish to protest against the doctrine that these two factors stand over against one another as the positive and negative poles of human existence. In other words, I protest against the notion, that the study of the practical everyday problems of human life is without what we are pleased to call a culture value,—that in the proper study of those problems one is not able to see the operation of fundamental and eternal principles.

I shall readily agree that there is always a grave danger that the trivial and temporary objects of everyday life may be viewed and studied without reference to these fundamental principles. But this danger is certainly no greater than that the permanent and eternal truths be studied without reference to the actual, concrete, workaday world in which we live. I have seen exercises in manual training that had for their purpose the perfection of the pupil in some little art of joinery for which he would, in all probability, have not the slightest use in his later life. But even if he should find use for it, the process was not being taught in the proper way. He was being made conscious only of the little trivial thing, and no part of his instruction was directed toward the much more important, fundamental lesson,—the lesson, namely, that "a little thing may be perfect, but that perfection itself is not a little thing."

I say that I have witnessed such an exercise in the very practical field of manual training. I may add that I went through several such exercises myself, and emerged with a disgust that always recurs to me when I am told that every boy will respond to the stimulus of the hammer and the jack plane. But I should hasten to add that I have also seen what we call the humanities so taught that the pupil has emerged from them with a supreme contempt for the life of labor and a feeling of disgust at the petty and trivial problems of human life which every one must face. I have seen art and literature so taught as to leave their students not with the high purpose to mold their lives in accordance with the high ideals that art and literature represent, not the firm resolution to do what they could to relieve the ugliness of the world where they found it ugly, or to do what they could to ennoble life when they found it vile; but rather with an attitude of calm superiority, as if they were in some way privileged to the delights of æsthetic enjoyment, leaving the baser born to do the world's drudgery.

I have seen the principles of agriculture so taught as to leave with the student the impression that he could raise more corn than his neighbor and sell it at a higher price if he mastered the principles of nitrification; and all without one single reference to the basic principle of conservation upon which the welfare of the human race for all time to come must inevitably depend,—without a single reference to the moral iniquity of waste and sloth and ignorance. But I have also seen men who have mastered the scientific method,—the method of controlled observation, and unprejudiced induction and inference,—in the laboratories of pure science; and who have gained so overweening and hypertrophied a regard for this method that they have considered it too holy to be contaminated by application to practical problems,—who have sneered contemptuously when some adventurer has proposed, for example, to subject the teaching of science itself to the searchlight of scientific method.

I trust that these examples have made my point clear, for it is certainly simple enough. If vocational education means simply that the arts and skills of industrial life are to be transmitted safely from generation to generation, a minimum of educational machinery is all that is necessary, and we do not need to worry much about it. If vocational education means simply this, it need not trouble us much; for economic conditions will sooner or later provide for an effective means of transmission, just as economic conditions will sooner or later perfect, through a blind and empirical process of elimination, the most effective methods of agriculture, as in the case of China and other overpopulated nations of the Orient.

But I take it that we mean by vocational education something more than this, just as we mean by cultural education something more than a veneer of language, history, pure science, and the fine arts. In the former case, the practical problems of life are to be lifted to the plane of fundamental principles; in the latter case, fundamental principles are to be brought down to the plane of present, everyday life. I can see no discrepancy here. To my mind there is no cultural subject that has not its practical outcome, and there is no practical subject that has not its humanizing influence if only we go to some pains to seek it out. I do not object to a subject of instruction that promises to put dollars into the pockets of those that study it. I do object to the mode of teaching that subject which fails to use this effective economic appeal in stimulating a glimpse of the broader vision. I do not object to the subject that appeals to the pupil's curiosity because it informs him of the wonderful deeds that men have done in the past. I do object to that mode of teaching this subject which simply arouses interest in a spectacular deed, and then fails to use this interest in the interpretation of present problems. I do not contend that in either case there must be an explicit pointing of morals and drawing of lessons. But I do contend that the teacher who is in charge of the process should always have this purpose in the forefront of his consciousness, and—now by direct comparison, now by indirection and suggestion—guide his pupils to the goal desired.

I hope that through careful tests, we shall some day be able to demonstrate that there is much that is good and valuable on both sides of every controverted educational question. After all, in this complex and intricate task of teaching to which you and I are devoting our lives, there is too much at stake to permit us for a moment to be dogmatic,—to permit us for a moment to hold ourselves in any other attitude save one of openness and reception to the truth when the truth shall have been demonstrated. Neither your ideas nor mine, nor those of any man or group of men, living or dead, are important enough to stand in the way of the best possible accomplishment of that great task to which we have set our hands.

IV

But I did not propose this morning to talk to you about science as a part of our educational curriculum, but rather about the scientific spirit and the scientific method as effective instruments for the solution of our own peculiar educational problems. I have tried to give you reasons for believing that an adoption of this policy does not necessarily commit us to materialism or to a narrowly economic point of view. I have attempted to show that the scientific method may be applied to the solution of our problems while we still retain our faith in ideals; and that, unless we do retain that faith, our investigations will be without point or meaning.

This problem of vocational education to which I have just referred is one that is likely to remain unsolved until we have made a searching investigation of its factors in the light of scientific method. Some people profess not to be worried by the difficulty of finding time in our elementary and secondary schools for the introduction of the newer subjects making for increased vocational efficiency. They would cut the Gordian knot with one single operation by eliminating enough of the older subjects to make room for the new. I confess that this solution does not appeal to me. Fundamentally the core of the elementary curriculum must, I believe, always be the arts that are essential to every one who lives the social life. In other words, the language arts and the number arts are, and always must be, the fundamentals of elementary education. I do not believe that specialized vocational education should ever be introduced at the expense of thorough training in the subjects that already hold their place in the curriculum. And yet we are confronted by the economic necessity of solving in some way this vocational problem. How are we to do it?

It is here that the scientific method may perhaps come to our aid. The obvious avenue of attack upon this problem is to determine whether we cannot save time and energy, not by the drastic operation of eliminating old subjects, but rather by improving our technique of teaching, so that the waste may be reduced, and the time thus saved given to these new subjects that are so vociferously demanding admission. In Cleveland, for example, the method of teaching spelling has been subjected to a rigid scientific treatment, and, as a result, spelling is being taught to-day vastly better than ever before and with a much smaller expenditure of time and energy. It has been due, very largely, to the application of a few well-known principles which the science of psychology has furnished.

Now that is vastly better than saying that spelling is a subject that takes too much time in our schools and consequently ought forthwith to be eliminated. In all of our school work enough time is undoubtedly wasted to provide ample opportunity for training the child thoroughly in some vocation if we wish to vocationalize him, and I do not think that this would hurt him, even if he does not follow the vocation in later life.

To-day we are attempting to detect these sources of waste in technique. The problems of habit building or memorizing are already well on the way to solution. Careful tests have shown the value of doing memory work in a certain definite way—learning by unit wholes rather than by fragments, for example. Experiments have been conducted to determine the best length of time to give to drill processes, such as spelling, and penmanship, and the fundamental tables of arithmetic. It is already clearly demonstrated that brief periods of intense concentration are more economical than longer periods during which the monotony of repetition fags the mind to a point where it can no longer work effectively. We are also beginning to see from these tests, that a systematic method of attacking such a problem as the memorizing of the tables will do much to save time and promote efficiency. We are finding that it is extremely profitable to instruct children in the technique of learning,—to start them out in the right way by careful example, so that much of the time and energy that was formerly dissipated, may now be conserved.

And there is a suggestion, also, that in the average school, the vast possibilities of the child's latent energy are only imperfectly realized. A friend of mine stumbled accidentally upon this fact by introducing a new method of grading. He divided his pupils into three groups or streams. The group that progressed the fastest was made up of those who averaged 85 per cent and over in their work. A middle group averaged between 75 per cent and 85 per cent in their work, and a third, slow group was made up of those who averaged below 75 per cent. At the end of the first month, he found that a certain proportion of his pupils, who had formerly hovered around the passing grade of 70, began to forge ahead. Many of them easily went into the fastest stream, but they were still satisfied with the minimum standing for that group. In other words, whether we like to admit it or not, most men and women and boys and girls are content with the passing grades, both in school and in life. So common is the phenomenon that we think of the matter fatalistically. But supply a stimulus, raise the standard, and you will find some of these individuals forging up to the next level.

Professor James's doctrine of latent energies bids fair to furnish the solution of a vast number of perplexing educational problems. Certain it is that our pupils of to-day are not overburdened with work. They are sometimes irritated by too many tasks, sometimes dulled by dead routine, sometimes exhilarated to the point of mental *ennui* by spectacular appeals to immediate interest. But they are seldom overworked, or even worked to within a healthful degree of the fatigue point.

Elementary education has often been accused of transacting its business in small coin,—of dealing with and emphasizing trivialities,—and yet every time that the scientific method touches the field of education, it reveals the fundamental significance of little things. Whether the third-grade pupil should memorize the multiplication tables in the form, "8 times 9 equals 72" or simply "8-9's—72" seems a matter of insignificance in contrast with the larger problems that beset us. And yet scientific investigation tells us clearly and unequivocally that any useless addition to a formula to be memorized increases the time for reducing the formula to memory, and interferes significantly with its recall and application. It may seem a matter of trivial importance whether the pupil increases the subtrahend number or decreases the minuend number when he subtracts digits that involve taking or borrowing; and yet investigation proves that to increase the subtrahend number is by far the simpler process, and eliminates both a source of waste and a source of error, which, in the aggregate, may assume a significance to mental economy that is well worth considering.

In fact, if we are ever to solve the broader, bigger, more attractive problems,—like the problem of vocational education, or the problem of retardation,—we must first find a solution for some of the smaller and seemingly trivial questions of the very existence of which the lay public may be quite unaware, but which you and I know to mean an untold total of waste and inefficiency in the work that we are trying to do.

And one reason why the scientific attitude toward educational problems appeals to me is simply because this attitude carries with it a respect for these seemingly trivial and commonplace problems; for just as the greatest triumph of the teaching art is to get our pupils to see in those things of life that are fleeting and transitory the operation of fundamental and eternal principles, so the glory of the scientific method lies in its power to reveal the significance of the commonplace and to teach us that no slightest detail of our daily work is necessarily devoid of inspiration; that every slightest detail of school method and school management has a meaning and a significance that it is worth our while to ponder.

CHAPTER VIII

THE POSSIBILITY OF TRAINING CHILDREN HOW TO STUDY[14]

I

In its widest aspects, the problem of teaching pupils how to study forms a large part of the larger educational problem. It means, not only teaching them how to read books, and to make the content of books part of their own mental capital, but also, and perhaps far more significantly, teaching them how to draw lessons from their own experiences; not only how to observe and classify and draw conclusions, but also how to evaluate their experience—how to judge whether certain things that they do give adequate or inadequate results.

In the narrower sense, however, the art of study may be said to consist in the ability to assimilate the experiences of others, and it is in this narrower sense that I shall discuss the problem to-day. It is not only in books that human experience is recorded, and yet it is true that the reading of books is the most economical means of gaining these experiences; consequently, we may still further narrow our problem to this: How may pupils be trained effectively to glean, through the medium of the printed page, the great lessons of race experience?

The word "study" is thus used in the sense in which most teachers employ it. When we speak of a pupil's studying his lessons, we commonly mean that he is bending over a text-book, attempting to assimilate the contents of the text. Just what it means to study, even in this narrow sense of the term,—just what it means, psychologically, to assimilate even the simplest thoughts of others,—I cannot tell you, and I do not know of any one who can answer this seemingly simple question satisfactorily. We all study, but what happens in our minds when we do study is a mystery. We all do some thinking, and yet the psychology of thinking is the great undiscovered and unexplored region in the field of mental science. Until we know something of the psychology of thinking, we can hope for very little definite information concerning the psychology of study, for study is so intimately bound up with thinking that the two are not to be separated.

But even if it is impossible at the present time to analyze the process of studying, we are pretty well agreed as to what constitutes successful study, and many rules have been formulated for helping pupils to acquire effective habits of study. These rules concern us only indirectly at the present time, for our problem is still

[14] A paper read before the Superintendents' Section of the Illinois State Teachers' Association, December 29, 1910.

narrower in its scope. It has to do with the possibility of so training children in the art of study, not only that they may study effectively in school, but also that they may carry over the habits and methods of study thus acquired into the tasks of later life. In other words, the topic that we are discussing is but one phase of the problem of formal discipline,—the problem of securing a transfer of training from a specific field to other fields; and my purpose is to view this topic of "study" in the light of what we know concerning the possibilities of transfer.

Let me take a specific example. I am not so much concerned with the problem of getting a pupil to master a history lesson quickly and effectively,—not how he may best assimilate the facts concerning the Missouri Compromise, for example. My task is rather to determine how we can make his mastery of the Missouri Compromise a lesson in the general art of study,—how that mastery may help him develop what we used to call the general power of study,—the capacity to apply an effective method of study to other problems, perhaps, very far removed from the history lesson; in other words, how that single lesson may help him in the more general task of finding any type of information when he needs it, of assimilating it once he has found it, and of applying it once he has assimilated it.

In an audience of practical teachers, it is hardly necessary to emphasize the significance of doing this very thing. From one point of view, it may be asserted that the whole future of what we term general education, as distinguished from technical or vocational education, depends upon our ability to solve problems like this, and solve them satisfactorily. We can never justify universal general education beyond the merest rudiments unless we can demonstrate acceptably that the training which general education furnishes will help the individual to solve the everyday problems of his life. Either we must train the pupil in a general way so that he will be able to acquire specialized skill more quickly and more effectively than will the pupil who lacks this general training; or we must give up a large part of the general-culture courses that now occupy an important part in our elementary and secondary curriculums, and replace these with technical and vocational subjects that shall have for their purpose the development of specialized efficiency.

All teachers, I take it, are alive to the grave dangers of the latter policy. Whether we have thought the matter through logically or not we certainly *feel* strongly that too early specialization will work a serious injury to the cause of education, and, through education, to the larger cause of social advancement and enlightenment. We view with grave foreboding any policy that will shut the door of opportunity to any child, no matter how humble or how unpromising. And yet we also know that, unless the general education that we now offer can be distinctly shown to have a beneficial influence upon specialized efficiency, we shall be forced by economic conditions into this very policy. It is small wonder, then, that so many of our educational discussions and investigations to-day turn upon this problem; and among the various phases of the problem none is more significant than that which is covered by our topic of to-day,—How may we develop in the pupil a general power or capacity for gaining information independently of schools and teachers? If we could adequately develop this power, there is much in the way of specialized instruction that could be safely left to the individual himself. If we could teach him how to study, then we could perhaps trust him to master some of the principles of any calling that he undertakes in so far as these principles can be mastered from books. To teach the child to study effectively is to do the most useful thing that could be done to help him to adjust himself to any environment of modern civilized life into which he may be thrown. For there is one thing that the more radical advocates of a narrow vocational education commonly forget, and that is the constant change that is going on in industrial processes. When we limit our vocational teaching to a mere mastery of technique, there is no guarantee that the process which we teach to-day may not be discarded in five or ten years from to-day. Even the narrower technical principles which are so extremely important to-day may be relatively insignificant by the time that the child whom we are training takes his place in the industrial world. But if we can arm the individual with the more fundamental principles which are fixed for all time; and if, in addition to this, we can teach him how to master the specialized principles which may come into the field unheralded and unexpected, and turn topsy-turvy the older methods of doing his work, then we shall have done much toward helping him in solving that perplexing problem of gaining a livelihood.

II

I shall not try in this discussion of the problem of study to summarize completely the principles and precepts that have been presented so well in the four books on the subject that have appeared in the last two years. I do not know, in fact, of any book that is more useful to the teacher just at present than Professor Frank McMurry's *How to Study and Teaching how to Study*. It is a book that is both a help and a delight, for it is clear and well-organized, and written in a vivacious style and with a wealth of concrete illustration that holds the attention from beginning to end. The chief fault that I have to find with it is the fault that I have to find with almost every educational book that comes from the press to-day,—the tendency, namely, to imply that the teacher of to-day is doing very little to solve these troublesome problems. As a matter of fact, many teachers are securing excellent results from their attempts to teach pupils how to study. Otherwise we should not find so many energetic young men to-day who are making an effective individual mastery of the principles of their respective trades and professions independently of schools and teachers. Our attitude toward these questions, far from being that of the pessimist, should be that of the optimist. Our task should be to seek out these successful teachers, and find out how they do their work.

Among the most important points emphasized by the recent writers upon the art of study is the necessity for some form of motivation in the work of mastering the text. We all know that if a pupil feels a distinct need for getting information out of a book, the chances are that he will get it if the book is available and if he can read. To create a problem that will involve in its solution the gaining of such information is, therefore, one of the best approaches to a mastery of the art of study. It is, however, only the beginning. It furnishes the necessary energy, but does not map out the path along which this energy is to be expended. And this is where the greater emphasis, perhaps, is needed.

One of the best teachers that I ever knew taught the subject that we now call agronomy,—a branch of agricultural science that has to do with field crops. I was a mere boy when I sat under his instruction, but certain points in his method of teaching made a most distinct impression upon me. Lectures we had, of course, for lecturing was the orthodox method of class instruction. But this man did something more than merely lecture. He assigned each one of his students a plat of ground on the college farm. Upon this plat of ground, a definite experiment was to be conducted. One of my experiments had to do with the smut of oats. I was to try the effect of treating the seed with hot water in order to see whether it would prevent the fungus from later destroying the ripening grain. The very nature of the problem interested me intensely. I began to wonder about the life-history of this fungus,—how it looked and how it germinated and how it grew and wrought its destructive influence. It was not long before I found myself spending some of my leisure moments in the library trying to find out what was known concerning this subject. I was not so successful as I might have been, but I am confident that I learned more about parasitic fungi under the spur of that curiosity than I should have done in five times the number of hours spent in formal, meaningless study.

But the point of my experience is not that a problem interest had been awakened, but rather that the white heat of that interest was not utilized so completely as it might have been utilized in fixing upon my mind some important details in the general method of running down references and acquiring information. That was the moment to strike, and one serious defect of our school organization to-day is that most teachers, like my teacher at that time, have so much to do that anything like individual attention at such moments is out of the question.

Next to individual attention, probably, the best way to overcome the difficulty is to give class instruction in these matters,—to set aside a definite period for teaching pupils the technique of using books. If one could arouse a sufficiently general problem interest, this sort of instruction could be made most effective. But even if the problem interest is not general, I think that it is well to assume that it exists in some pupils, at least, and to give them the benefit of class instruction in the art of study,—even if some of the seed should fall upon barren soil.

This aspect of teaching pupils how to study is particularly important in the upper grades and the high school, where pupils have sufficiently mastered the technique of reading to be intrusted with individual problems, and where some reference books are commonly available. Chief among these always is the dictionary, and to get pupils to use this ponderous volume effectively is one of the important steps in teaching them how to study. Here, too, it is easy to be pedantic. As I shall insist strenuously a little later, the chief factor in insuring a transfer of training from one subject to another is to leave in the pupil's mind a distinct consciousness that the method that he has been trained to follow is worth while,—that it gets results. The dictionary habit is likely to begin and end within the schoolroom unless steps are taken to insure the operation of this factor. It is easy to overwork the dictionary and to use it fruitlessly, in so great a measure, in fact, that the pupil will never want to see a dictionary again.

Aside from the use of the dictionary, is the use of the helps that modern books provide for finding the information that may be desired,—indices, tables of contents, marginal and cross-references, and the like. These, again, are most significant in the work of the upper grades and the high school, and here again if we wish the skill that is developed in their use to be transferred, we must take pains to see that the pupil really appreciates their value,—that he realizes their time-saving and energy-saving functions. I do not know that there is any better way to do this than to let him flounder around without them for a little so that his sense of their value may be enhanced by contrast.

III

Another important step emphasized by the recent writers is the need for training children to pick out the significant features in the text or portion of the text that they are reading. This, of course, is work that is to be undertaken from the very moment that they begin to use books. How to do it effectively is a puzzling problem and one that will amply repay study and experimentation by the individual teacher. Much studying of lessons by teachers and pupils together will help, provided that the exercise is spirited and vital, and is not looked upon by the pupils as an easy way of getting out of recitation work. McMurry strongly recommends the marking of books to indicate the topic sentences and the other salient features. Personally, I am sure from my own experience that the assignment is all-important here, and that study questions and problems which can be answered or solved by reference to the text will help matters very much; but care must, of course, be taken that the continued use of such questions does not preclude the pupil's own mastery of the art of study. To eliminate this danger, it is well that the pupils be requested frequently to make out their own lists of questions, and, as speedily as possible, both the questions made by the pupil and those made by the teacher, should be replaced by topical outlines. By taking care that the questions are logically arranged,—that is, that a general question refer to the topic of the paragraph, and other subordinate questions to the subordinate details of the paragraph,—the transition from the questions to the topical outline may be readily made. Simultaneously with this will go the transition in recitation from the question-and-answer type to the topical type; and when you have trained a class into the habit of topical recitation,—when each pupil can talk right through a topic (not around it or underneath it or above it) without the use of "pumping" questions by the teacher,—you have gone a long way toward developing the art of study.

The transfer of this training, however, is quite another matter. There are pupils who can work up excellent topical recitations from their school text-books but who are utterly at sea in getting a grasp on a subject treated in other books. Here again the problem lies in getting the pupil to see the method apart from its content, and to show him that it really brings results that are worth while. If, in our training in the topical method, we are too formal and didactic, the art of study will begin and end right there. It is here that the factor of motivation is of supreme importance. When real problems are raised which require for their solution intelligent reading, the general worth of the method of study can be clearly shown. I do not go so far as to say that the pupil should never be required to study unless he has a real problem that he wishes to solve. In fact, I think that we still have a large place for the formal, systematic mastery of texts by every pupil in our schools. I do contend, however, that the frequent introduction of real problems will give us an opportunity to show the pupil that the method that he has utilized in his more formal school work is adequate and essential to do the thing that appeals to him as worth while. Only in this way, I believe, can we insure that transfer of training which is the important factor from our present standpoint.

And I ought also to say, parenthetically, that we should not interpret too narrowly this word "motivation." Let us remember that what may appeal to the adult as an effective motive does not always appeal to the child as such. Economic motives are the most effective, probably, in our own adult lives, and probably very effective with high-school pupils, but economic motives are not always strong in young children, nor should we wish them to be. It is not always true that the child will approach a school task sympathetically when he knows that the task is an essential preparation for the life that is going on about him. He may work harder at a task in order to get ahead of his fellow-pupils than he would if the motive were to fit him to enter a shop or a factory. Motive is largely a matter of instinct with the child, and he may, indeed, be perfectly satisfied with a school task just as it stands. For example, we all know that children enjoy the right kind of drill. Repetition, especially rhythmic repetition, is instinctive,—it satisfies an inborn need. Where such a condition exists, it is an obvious waste of time to search about for more indirect motives. The economical thing to do is to turn the ready energy of the child into the channel that is already open to it, so long as this procedure fits in with the results that we must secure. I feel like emphasizing this fact, inasmuch as the terms "problem interest" and "motivation" seem most commonly to be associated in the minds of teachers with what we adults term "real" or economic situations. To learn a lesson well may often be a sufficient motive,—may often constitute a "real" situation to the child,—and if it does, it will serve very effectively our purposes in this other task,—namely, getting the pupil to see the worth of the method that we ask him to employ.

IV

There are one or two points of a general nature in connection with the art of study that should be emphasized. In the first place, the upper-grade and high-school pupils are, I believe, mature enough to appreciate in some degree what knowledge really means. One of the fallacies of which I was possessed on completing my work in the lower schools was the belief that there are some men who know everything. I naturally concluded that the superintendent of schools was one of these men; the family physician was another; the leading man in my town was a third; and any one who ever wrote a book was put, *ex officio* so to speak, into this class without further inquiry. One of the most astounding revelations of my later education was to learn that, after all, the amount of real knowledge in this world, voluminous though it seems, is after all pitiably small. Of opinion and speculation we have a surplus, but of real, downright, hard fact, our capital is still most insignificant. And I wonder if something could not be done in the high school to teach pupils the difference between fact and opinion, and something also of the slow, laborious process through which real facts are accumulated. How many mistakes of life are due to the lack of the judicial attitude right here. What mistakes we all make when we try to evaluate writings outside of our own special field of knowledge or activity. Nothing depresses me to-day quite so much as the readiness with which laymen mistake opinion for fact in the field of psychology and education,—and I suppose that my own hasty acceptance of statements in other fields would have a similar effect upon the specialists of those fields.

Can general education help us out at all in this matter? I have only one or two suggestions to make, and even these may not be worth a great deal. In the recent Polar controversy, the sympathies of the general public were, I think, at the outset with Cook. This was perhaps, natural, and yet the trained mind ought to have withheld judgment for one reason if for no other,—and that one reason was Peary's long Arctic service, his unquestioned mastery of the technique of polar travel, his general reputation for honesty and caution in advancing opinions. By all the lessons that history teaches, Peary's word should have had precedence over Cook's, for Peary was a specialist, while Cook was only an amateur. And yet the general public discounted entirely those lessons, and trusted rather the novice, with what results it is now unnecessary to review,—and in nine cases out of ten, the results will be the same.

Could we not, as part of our work in training pupils to study, also teach them to give some sort of an evaluation to the authorities that they consult? Could we not teach them that, in nine cases out of ten, at least, the man who has the message most worth listening to is the man who has worked the hardest and the longest in his field, and who enjoys the best reputation among his fellow-workers? Sometimes, I admit, the rule does not work, and especially with men whose reputations as authorities have outlived their period of productivity, but even this mistake could be guarded against. Certainly high-school pupils ought distinctly to understand that the authors of their text-books are not always the most learned men or the greatest authorities in the fields that they treat. The use of biographical dictionaries, of the books that are appearing in various fields giving brief biographies and often some authoritative estimate of the workers in these fields, is important in this connection.

McMurry recommends that pupils be encouraged to take a critical attitude toward the principles they are set to master,—to judge, as he says, the soundness and worth of the statements that they learn. This is certainly good advice, and wherever the pupil can intelligently deal with real sources, it is well frequently to have him check up the statements of secondary sources. But, after all, this is the age of the specialist, and to trust one's untrained judgment in a field remote from one's knowledge and experience is likely to lead to unfortunate results. We have all sorts of illustrations from the ignorant man who will not trust the physician or the health official in matters of sanitation; because he lacks the proper perspective, he jumps to the conclusion that the specialist is a fraud. Would it not be well to supplement McMurry's suggestion by the one that I have just made,—that is, that we train pupils how to evaluate authorities as well as facts,—how to protect themselves from the quack and the faker who live like parasites upon the ignorance of laymen, both in medicine, in education, and in Arctic exploration?

And I believe that there is a place, also, in the high school, especially in connection with the work in science and history, for giving pupils some idea of how knowledge is really gained. I should not teach science exclusively by the laboratory method, nor history exclusively by the source method, but I should certainly take frequent opportunity to let pupils work through some simple problems from the beginnings, struggling with the conditions somewhat as the discoverers themselves struggled; following up "blind leads" and toilsomely returning for a fresh start; meeting with discouragement; and finally feeling, perhaps, some of the joy that comes with success after struggle; and all in order that they may know better and appreciate more fully the cost and the worth of that intellectual heritage which the master-minds of the world have bequeathed to the present and the future. And along with this, as they master the principles of science, let them learn also the human side of science,—the story of Newton, withholding his great discovery for years until he could be absolutely certain that it was a law; until he could get the very commonplace but obstreperous moon into harmony with his law of falling bodies;—the story of Darwin, with his twenty-odd years of the most patient and persistent kind of toil; delving into the most unpromising materials, reading the driest books, always on the lookout for the facts that would point the way to the explanation of species;—the story of Morse and his bitter struggle against poverty, and sickness, and innumerable disappointments up to the time when, in advancing years, success crowned his efforts.

All this may seem very remote from the prosaic task of teaching pupils how to study; and yet it will lend its influence toward the attainment of that end. For, after all, we must lead our pupils to see that some books, in spite of their formidable difficulties and their apparent abstractions, are still close to life, and that the truth which lies in books, and which we wish them to assimilate, has been wrought out of human experience, and not brought down miraculously from some remote storehouse of wisdom that is accessible only to the elect. We poke a good deal of fun at book learning nowadays, and there is a pedantic type of book learning that certainly deserves all the ridicule that can be heaped upon it. But it is not wise to carry satire and ridicule too far in any direction, and especially when it may mean creating in young minds a distrust of the force that, more than any other single factor, has operated to raise man above the savage.

V

To teach the child the art of study means, then, that we take every possible occasion to impress upon his mind the value of study as a means of solving real and vital problems, and that, with this as an incentive, we gradually and persistently and systematically lead him to grasp the method of study as a method,—that is, slowly and gradually to abstract the method from the particular cases to which he applies it and to emotionalize it,—to make it an ideal. Only in this way, so far as we may know, can the art be so generalized as to find ready application in his later life. To this end, it is essential that the steps be taken repeatedly,—not begun to-day and never thought of again until next year,—but daily, even hourly, insuring a little growth. This means, too, not only that the teacher must possess a high degree of patience,—that first principle of pedagogic skill,—but also that he have a comprehensive grasp of the problem, and the ability to separate the woods from the trees, so that, to him at least, the chief aim will never be lost to view.

But, even at its best, the task is a severe one, and we need, here as elsewhere in education, carefully controlled tests and experiments, that will enable us to get at the facts. Above all, let me protest against the incidental theory of teaching pupils how to study. To adopt the incidental policy in any field of education,—whether in arithmetic, or spelling, or reading; whether in developing the power of reasoning or the memory, or the art of study,—is to throw wide open the doors that lead to the lines of least resistance, to lax methods, to easy honors, to weakened mental fiber, and to scamped work. Just as the pernicious doctrine of the subconscious is the first and last refuge of the psycho-faker, so incidental learning is the first and last refuge of soft pedagogy. And I mean by incidental learning, going at a teaching task in an indolent, unreflective, hit-or-miss fashion in the hope that somehow or other from this process will emerge the very definite results that we desire.

CHAPTER IX

A PLEA FOR THE DEFINITE IN EDUCATION[15]

I

One way to be definite in education is to formulate as clearly as we can the aims that we hope to realize in every stage of our work. The task of teaching is so complex that, unless we strive earnestly and persistently to reduce it to the simplest possible terms, we are bound to work blindly and ineffectively.

It is only one phase of this topic that I wish to discuss with you this morning. My plea for the definite in education will be limited not only to the field of educational aims and values, but to a small corner of that field. Your morning's program has dealt with the problem of teaching history in the elementary school. I should like, if you are willing, to confine my remarks to this topic, and to attack the specific question, What is the history that we teach in the grades to do for the pupil? I wish to make this limitation, not only because what I have to say will be related to the other topics on the program, but also because this very subject of history is one which the lack of a definite standard of educational value has been keenly felt.

I should admit at the outset that my interest in history is purely educational. I have had no special training in historical research. As you may perhaps infer from my discussion, my acquaintance with historical facts is very far from comprehensive. I speak as a layman in history,—and I do it openly and, perhaps, a little defiantly, for I believe that the last person to pass adequate judgment upon the general educational value of a given department of knowledge is a man who has made the department a life study. I have little faith in what the mathematician has to say regarding the educational value of mathematics *for the average elementary pupil,* because he is a special pleader and his conclusions cannot escape the coloring of his prejudice. I once knew an enthusiastic brain specialist who maintained that, in every grade of the elementary school, instruction should be required in the anatomy of the human brain. That man was an expert in his own line. He knew more about the structure of the brain than any other living man. But knowing more about brain morphology also implied that he knew less about many other things, and among the things that he knew little about were the needs and capacities of children in the elementary school. He was a special pleader; he had been dealing with his special subject so long that it had assumed a disproportionate value in his eyes. Brain morphology had given him fame, honor, and worldly emoluments.

[15] An address delivered March 18, 1910, before the Central Illinois Teachers' Association.

Naturally he would have an exaggerated notion of its value.

It is the same with any other specialist. As specialists in education, you and I are likely to overemphasize the importance of the common school in the scheme of creation. Personally I am convinced that the work of elementary education is the most profoundly significant work in the world; and yet I can realize that I should be no fit person to make comparisons if the welfare of a number of other professions and callings were at stake. I should let an unbiased judge make the final determination.

II

The first question for which we should seek an answer in connection with the value of any school subject is this: How does it influence conduct? Let me insist at the outset that we cannot be definite by saying simply that we teach history in order to impart instruction. If there is one thing upon which we are all agreed to-day it is this: that it is what our pupils do that counts, not what they know. The knowledge that they may possess has value only in so far as it may directly or indirectly be turned over into action.

Let us not be mistaken upon this point. Knowledge is of the utmost importance, but it is important only as a means to an end—and the end is conduct. If my pupils act in no way more efficiently after they have received my instruction than they would have acted had they never come under my influence, then my work as a teacher is a failure. If their conduct is less efficient, then my work is not only a failure,—it is a catastrophe. The knowledge that I impart may be absolutely true; the interest that I arouse may be intense; the affection that my pupils have for me may be genuine; but all these are but means to an end, and if the end is not attained, the means have been futile.

We have faith that the materials which we pour in at the hopper of sense impression will come out sooner or later at the spout of reaction, transformed by some mysterious process into efficient conduct. While the machinery of the process, like the mills of the gods, certainly grinds slowly, it is some consolation to believe that, at any rate, it *does* grind; and we are perhaps fain to believe that the exceeding fineness of the grist is responsible for our failure to detect at the spout all of the elements that we have been so careful to pour in at the hopper. What I should like to do is to examine this grinding process rather carefully,—to gain, if possible, some definite notion of the kind of grist we should like to produce, and then to see how the machinery may be made to produce this grist, and in what proportions we must mix the material that we pour into the hopper in order to gain the desired result.

I have said that we must ask of every subject that we teach, How does it influence conduct? Now when we ask this question concerning history a variety of answers are at once proposed. One group of people will assert that the facts of history have value because they can be directly applied to the needs of contemporary life. History, they will tell us, records the experiences of the race, and if we are to act intelligently we must act upon the basis of this experience. History informs us of the mistakes that former generations have made in adjusting themselves to the world. If we know history, we can avoid these mistakes. This type of reasoning may be said to ascribe a utilitarian value to the study of history. It assumes that historical knowledge is directly and immediately applicable to vital problems of the present day.

Now the difficulty with this value, as with many others that seem to have the sanction of reason, is that it does not possess the sanction of practical test. While knowledge doubtless affects in some way the present policy of our own government, it would be very hard to prove that the influence is in any way a direct influence. It is extremely doubtful whether the knowledge that the voters have of the history of their country will be recalled and applied at the ballot box next November. I do not say that the study of history that has been going on in the common schools for a generation will be entirely without effect upon the coming election. I simply maintain that this influence will be indirect,—but I believe that it will be none the less profound. One's vote at the next election will be determined largely by immediate and present conditions. But the way in which one interprets these conditions cannot help being profoundly influenced by one's historical study or lack of such study.

If it is clear, then, that the study of history cannot be justified upon a purely utilitarian basis, we may pass to the consideration of other values that have been proposed. The specialist in history, whose right to legislate upon this matter I have just called into question, will probably emphasize the disciplinary value of this study. Specialists are commonly enthusiastic over the disciplinary value of their special subjects. Their own minds have been so well developed by the pursuit of their special branches that they are impelled to recommend the same discipline for all minds. Again, we must not blame the specialist in history, for you and I think the same about our own special type of activity.

From the disciplinary point of view, the study of history is supposed to give one the mastery of a special method of reasoning. Historical method involves, above all else, the careful sifting of evidence, the minutest scrutiny of sources in order to judge whether or not the records are authentic, and the utmost care in coming to conclusions. Now it will be generally agreed that these are desirable types of skill to possess whether one is an historian or a lawyer or a teacher or a man of business. And yet, as in all types of discipline, the difficulty lies, not so much in acquiring the specific skill, as in transferring the skill thus acquired to other fields of activity. Skill of any sort is made up of a multitude of little specific habits, and it is a current theory that habit functions effectively only in the specific situation in which it has been built up, or in situations closely similar. But whether this is true or not it is obvious that the teaching of elementary history provides very few opportunities for this type of training.

A third view of the way in which historical knowledge is thought to work into action may be discussed under the head of the cultural value. History, like literature, is commonly assumed to give to the individual who studies it, a certain amount of that commodity which the world calls culture. Precisely what culture consists in, no one, apparently, is ready to tell us, but we all admit that it is real, if not tangible and definable, nor can we deny that the individual who possesses culture conducts himself, as a rule, differently from the individual who does not possess it. In other words, culture is a practical thing, for the only things that are practical are the things that modify or control human action.

It is doubtless true that the study of history does add to this intangible something that we call "culture," but the difficulty with this value lies in the fact that, even after we have accepted it as valid, we are in no way better off regarding our methods. Like many other theories, its truth is not to be denied, but its truth gives us no inkling of a solution of our problem. What we need is an educational value of history, the recognition of which will enable us to formulate a method for realizing the value.

III

The unsatisfactory character of these three values that have been proposed for history—the utilitarian, the disciplinary, and the cultural—is typical of the values that have been proposed for other subjects. Unless the aim of teaching any given subject can be stated in definite terms, the teacher must work very largely in the dark; his efforts must be largely of the "hit-or-miss" order. The desired value may be realized under these conditions, but, if it is realized, it is manifestly through accident, not through intelligent design. It is needless to point out the waste that such a blundering and haphazard adjustment entails. We all know how much of our teaching fails to hit the mark, even when we are clear concerning the result that we desire; we can only conjecture how much of the remainder fails of effect because we are hazy and obscure concerning its purpose.

Let us return to our original basic principle and see what light it may throw upon our problem. We have said that the efficiency of teaching must always be measured by the degree in which the pupil's conduct is modified. Taking conduct as our base, then, let us reason back and see what factors control conduct, and, if possible, how these "controls" may be influenced by the processes of education working through the lesson in history.

I shall start with a very simple and apparently trivial example. When I was living in the Far West, I came to know something of the Chinese, who are largely engaged, as you know, in domestic service in that part of the country. Most of the Chinese servants that I met corresponded very closely with what we read concerning Chinese character. We have all heard of the Chinese servant's unswerving adherence to a routine that he has once established. They say in the West that when a housewife gives her Chinese servant an object lesson in the preparation of a certain dish, she must always be very careful to make her demonstration perfect the first time. If, inadvertently, she adds one egg too many, she will find that, in spite of her protestations, the superfluous egg will always go into that preparation forever afterward. From what I know of the typical Oriental, I am sure that this warning is not overdrawn.

Now here is a bit of conduct, a bit of adjustment, that characterizes the Chinese cook. Not only that, but, in a general way, it is peculiar to all Chinese, and hence may be called a national trait. We might call it a vigorous national prejudice in favor of precedent. But whatever we call it, it is a very dominant force in Chinese life. It is the trait that, perhaps more than any other, distinguishes Chinese conduct from European or American conduct. Now one might think this trait to be instinctive,—to be bred in the bone rather than acquired,—but this I am convinced is not altogether true. At least one Chinese whom I knew did not possess it at all. He was born on a western ranch and his parents died soon after his birth. He was brought up with the children of the ranch owner, and is now a prosperous rancher himself. He lacks every characteristic that we commonly associate with the Chinese, save only the physical features. His hair is straight, his skin is saffron, his eyes are slightly aslant,—but that is all. As far as his conduct goes,—and that is the essential thing,—he is an American. In other words, his traits, his tendencies to action, are American and not Chinese. His life represents the triumph of environment over heredity.

When you visit England you find yourselves among a people who speak the same language that you speak,—or, perhaps it would be better to say, somewhat the same; at least you can understand each other. In a great many respects, the Englishman and the American are similar in their traits, but in a great many other respects they differ radically. You cannot, from your knowledge of American traits, judge what an Englishman's conduct will be upon every occasion. If you happened on Piccadilly of a rainy morning, for example, you would see the English clerks and storekeepers and professional men riding to their work on the omnibuses that thread their way slowly through the crowded thoroughfare. No matter how rainy the morning, these men would be seated on the tops of the omnibuses, although the interior seats might be quite unoccupied. No matter how rainy the morning, many of these men would be faultlessly attired in top hats and frock coats, and there they would sit through the drizzling rain, protecting themselves most inadequately with their opened umbrellas. Now there is a bit of conduct that you cannot find duplicated in any American city. It is a national habit,—or, perhaps, it would be better to say, it is an expression of a national trait,—and that national trait is a prejudice in favor of convention. It is the thing to do, and the typical Englishman does it, just as, when he is sent as civil governor to some lonely outpost in India, with no companions except scantily clad native servants, he always dresses conscientiously for dinner and sits down to his solitary meal clad in the conventional swallow-tail coat of civilization.

Now the way in which a Chinese cook prepares a custard, or the way in which an English merchant rides in an omnibus, may be trivial and unimportant matters in themselves, and yet, like the straw that shows which way the wind blows, they are indicative of vast and profound currents. The conservatism of the Chinese empire is only a larger and more comprehensive expression of the same trait or prejudice that leads the cook to copy literally his model. The present educational situation in England is only another expression of that same prejudice in favor of the established order, which finds expression in the merchant on the Piccadilly omnibus.

Whenever you pass from one country to another you will find this difference in tendencies to action. In Germany, for example, you will find something that amounts almost to a national fervor for economy and frugality. You will find it expressing itself in the care with which the German housewife does her marketing. You will find it expressing itself in the intensive methods of agriculture, through which scarcely a square inch of arable land is permitted to lie fallow,—through which, for example, even the shade trees by the roadside furnish fruit as well as shade, and are annually rented for their fruit value to industrious members of the community,—and it is said in one section of Germany that the only people known to steal fruit from these trees along the lonely country roads are American tourists, who, you will see, also have their peculiar standards of conduct. You will find this same fervor for frugality and economy expressing itself most extensively in that splendid forest policy by means of which the German states have conserved their magnificent timber resources.

But, whatever its expression, it is the same trait,—a trait born of generations of struggle with an unyielding soil, and yet a trait which, combined with the German fervor for science and education, has made possible the marvelous progress that Germany has made within the last half century.

What do we mean by national traits? Simply this: prejudices or tendencies toward certain typical forms of conduct, common to a given people. It is this community of conduct that constitutes a nation. A country whose people have different standards of action must be a divided country, as our own American history sufficiently demonstrates. Unless upon the vital questions of human adjustment, men are able to agree, they cannot live together in peace. If we are a distinctive and unique nation,—if we hold a distinctive and unique place among the nations of the globe,—it is because you and I and the other inhabitants of our country have developed distinctive and unique ideals and prejudices and standards, all of which unite to produce a community of conduct. And once granting that our national characteristics are worth while, that they constitute a distinct advance over the characteristics of the other nations of the earth, it becomes the manifest duty of the school to do its share in perpetuating these ideals and prejudices and standards. Once let these atrophy through disuse, once let them fail of transmission because of the decay of the home, or the decay of the school, or the decay of the social institutions that typify and express them, and our country must go the way of Greece and Rome, and, although our blood may thereafter continue pure and unmixed, and our physical characteristics may be passed on from generation to generation unchanged in form, our nation will be only a memory, and its history ancient history. Some of the Greeks of to-day are the lineal descendants of the Athenians and Spartans, but the ancient Greek standards of conduct, the Greek ideals, died twenty centuries ago, to be resurrected, it is true, by the renaissance, and to enjoy the glorious privilege of a new and wider sphere of life,—but among an alien people, and under a northern sun.

And so the true aim of the study of history in the elementary school is not the realization of its utilitarian, its cultural, or its disciplinary value. It is not a mere assimilation of facts concerning historical events, nor the memorizing of dates, nor the picturing of battles, nor the learning of lists of presidents,—although each of these factors has its place in fulfilling the function of historical study. The true function of national history in our elementary schools is to establish in the pupils' minds those ideals and standards of action which differentiate the American people from the rest of the world, and especially to fortify these ideals and standards by a description of the events and conditions through which they developed. It is not the facts of history that are to be applied to the problems of life; it is rather the emotional attitude, the point of view, that comes not from memorizing, but from appreciating, the facts. A mere fact has never yet had a profound influence over human conduct. A principle that is accepted by the head and not by the heart has never yet stained a battle field nor turned the tide of a popular election. Men act, not as they think, but as they feel, and it is not the idea, but the ideal, that is important in history.

IV

But what are the specific ideals and standards for which our nation stands and which distinguish, in a very broad but yet explicit manner, our conduct from the conduct of other peoples? If we were to ask this question of an older country, we could more easily obtain an answer, for in the older countries the national ideals have, in many cases, reached an advanced point of self-consciousness. The educational machinery of the German empire, for example, turns upon this problem of impressing the national ideals. It is one aim of the official courses of study, for instance, that history shall be so taught that the pupils will gain an overweening reverence for the reigning house of Hohenzollern. Nor is that newer ideal of national unity which had its seed sown in the Franco-Prussian War in any danger of neglect by the watchful eye of the government. Not only must the teacher impress it upon every occasion, but every attempt is also made to bring it daily fresh to the minds of the people through great monuments and memorials. Scarcely a hamlet is so small that it does not possess its Bismarck *Denkmal*, often situated upon some commanding hill, telling to each generation, in the sublime poetry of form, the greatness of the man who made German unity a reality instead of a dream.

But in our country, we do not thus consciously formulate and express our national ideals. We recognize them rather with averted face as the adolescent boy recognizes any virtue that he may possess, as if half-ashamed of his weakness. We have monuments to our heroes, it is true, but they are often inaccessible, and as often they fail to convey in any adequate manner, the greatness of the lessons which the lives of these heroes represent. Where Germany has a hundred or more impressive memorials to the genius of Bismarck, we have but one adequate memorial to the genius of Washington, while for Lincoln, who represents the typical American standards of life and conduct more faithfully than any other one character in our history, we have no memorial that is at all adequate,—and we should have a thousand. Some day our people will awake to the possibilities that inhere in these palpable expressions of the impalpable things for which our country stands. We shall come to recognize the vast educative importance of perpetuating, in every possible way, the deep truths that have been established at the cost of so much blood and treasure.

To embody our national ideals in the personages of the great figures of history who did so much to establish them is the most elementary method of insuring their conservation and transmission. We are beginning to appreciate the value of this method in our introductory courses of history in the intermediate and lower grammar grades. The historical study outlined for these grades in most of our state and city school programs includes mainly biographical materials. As long as the purpose of this study is kept steadily in view by the teacher, its value may be very richly realized. The danger lies in an obscure conception of the purpose. We are always too prone to teach history didactically, and to teach biographical history didactically is to miss the mark entirely. The aim here is not primarily instruction, but inspiration; not merely learning, but also appreciation. To tell the story of Lincoln's life in such a way that its true value will be realized requires first upon the part of the teacher a sincere appreciation of the great lesson of Lincoln's life. Lincoln typifies the most significant and representative of American ideals. His career stands for and illustrates the greatest of our national principles,—the principle of equality,—not the equality of birth, not the equality of social station, but the equality of opportunity. That a child of the lowliest birth, reared under conditions apparently the most unfavorable for rich development, limited by the sternest poverty, by lack of formal education, by lack of family pride and traditions, by lack of an environment of culture, by the hard necessity of earning his own livelihood almost from earliest childhood,—that such a man should attain to the highest station in the land and the proudest eminence in its history, and should have acquired from the apparently unfavorable environment of his early life the very qualities that made him so efficient in that station and so permanent in that eminence,—this is a miracle that only America could produce. It is this conception that the teacher must have, and this he must, in some measure, impress upon his pupils.

V

In the teaching of history in the elementary school, the biographical treatment is followed in the later grammar grades by a systematic study of the main events of American history. Here the method is different, but the purpose is the same. This purpose is, I take it, to show how our ideals and standards have developed, through what struggles and conflicts they have become firmly established; and the aim must be to have our pupils relive, as vividly as possible, the pain and the struggles and the striving and the triumph, to the end that they may appreciate, however feebly, the heritage that is theirs.

Here again it is not the facts as such that are important, but the emotional appreciation of the facts, and to this end, the coloring must be rich, the pictures vivid, the contrasts sharply drawn. The successful teacher of history has the gift of making real the past. His pupils struggle with Columbus against a frightened, ignorant, mutinous crew; they toil with the Pilgrim fathers to conquer the wilderness; they follow the bloody trail of the Deerfield victims through the forest to Canada; they too resist the encroachments of the Mother Country upon their rights as English citizens; they suffer through the long winter at Valley Forge and join with Washington in his midnight vigils; they rejoice at Yorktown; they dream with Jefferson and plead with Webster; their hearts are fired with the news of Sumter; they clinch their teeth at Bull Run; they gather hope at Donelson, but they shudder at Shiloh; they struggle through the Wilderness with Grant; tired but triumphant, they march home from Appomattox; and through it all, in virtue of the limitless capacities of vicarious experience, they have shared the agonies of Lincoln.

Professor Mace, in his essay on *Method in History*, tells us that there are two distinct phases to every historical event. These are the event itself and the human feeling that brought it forth. It has seemed to me that there are three phases,—the event itself, the feeling that brought it forth, and the feeling to which it gave birth; for no event is historically important unless it has transformed in some way the ideals and standards of the people,—unless it has shifted, in some way, their point of view, and made them act differently from the way in which they would have acted had the event never occurred. One leading purpose in the teaching of history is to show how ideals have been transformed, how we have come to have standards different from those that were once held.

Many of our national ideals have their roots deep down in English history. Not long ago I heard a seventh-grade class discussing the Magna Charta. It was a class in American history, and yet the events that the pupils had been studying occurred three centuries before the discovery of America. They had become familiar with the long list of abuses that led to the granting of the charter. They could tell very glibly what this great document did for the English people. They traced in detail the subsequent events that led to the establishment of the House of Commons. All this was American history just as truly as if the events described had occurred on American soil. They were gaining an appreciation of one of the most fundamental of our national ideals,—the ideal of popular government. And not only that, but they were studying popular government in its simplest form, uncomplicated by the innumerable details and the elaborate organizations which characterize popular government to-day.

And when these pupils come to the time when this ideal of self-government was transplanted to American soil, they will be ready to trace with intelligence the changes that it took on. They will appreciate the marked influence which geographical conditions exert in shaping national standards of action. How richly American history reveals and illustrates this influence we are only just now beginning to appreciate. The French and the English colonists developed different types of national character partly because they were placed under different geographical conditions. The St. Lawrence and the Great Lakes gave the French an easy means of access into the vast interior of the continent, and provided innumerable temptations to exploitation rather than a few incentives to development. Where the French influence was dispersed over a wide territory, the English influence was concentrated. As a consequence, the English energy went to the development of resources that were none too abundant, and to the establishment of permanent institutions that would conserve these resources. The barrier of the Appalachians hemmed them in,—three hundred miles of alternate ridge and valley kept them from the West until they were numerically able to settle rather than to exploit this country. Not a little credit for the ultimate English domination of the continent must be given to these geographical conditions.

But geography does not tell the whole story. The French colonists differed from the English colonists from the outset in standards of conduct. They had brought with them the principle of paternalism, and, in time of trouble, they looked to France for support. The English colonists brought with them the principle of self-reliance and, in time of trouble, they looked only to themselves. And so the old English ideals had a new birth and a broader field of application on American soil. There is nothing finer in our country's history than the attitude of the New England colonists during the intercolonial wars. Their northern frontier covering two hundred miles of unprotected territory was constantly open to the incursions of the French from Canada and their Indian allies, to appease whom the French organized their raids. And yet, so deeply implanted was this ideal of self-reliance that New England scarcely thought of asking aid of the mother country and would have protested to the last against the permanent establishment of a military garrison within her limits. For a period extending over fifty years, New England protected her own borders. She felt the terrors of savage warfare in its most sanguinary forms. And yet, uncomplaining, she taxed herself to repel the invaders. The people loved their own independence too much to part with it, even for the sake of peace, prosperity, and security. At a later date, unknown to the mother country, they raised and equipped from their own young men and at their own expense, the punitive expedition that, in the face of seemingly certain defeat, captured the French fortress at Louisburg, and gave to English military annals one of its most brilliant victories. To get the pupil to live through these struggles, to feel the impetus of idealism upon conduct, to appreciate what that almost forgotten half-century of conflict meant to the development of our national character, would be to realize the greatest value that colonial history can have for its students. It lays bare the source of that strength which made New England preëminent in the Revolution, and which has placed the mint mark of New England idealism upon the coin of American character. Could a pupil who has lived vicariously through such experiences as these easily forsake principle for policy?

A newspaper cartoon published a year or so ago, gives some notion of the danger that we are now facing of losing that idealism upon which our country was founded. The cartoon represents the signing of the Declaration of Independence. The worthies are standing about the table dressed in the knee breeches and flowing coats of the day, with wigs conventionally powdered and that stately bearing which characterizes the typical historical painting. John Hancock is seated at the table prepared to make his name immortal. A figure, however, has just appeared in the doorway. It is the cartoonist's conventional conception of the modern Captain of Industry. His silk hat is on the back of his head as if he had just come from his office as fast as his forty-horse-power automobile could carry him. His portly form shows evidences of intense excitement. He is holding his hand aloft to stay the proceedings, while from his lips comes the stage whisper: "Gentlemen, stop! You will hurt business!" What would those old New England fathers think, could they know that such a conception may be taken as representing a well-recognized tendency of the present day? And remember, too, that those old heroes had something of a passion for trade themselves.

But when we seek for the source of our most important national ideal,—the ideal that we have called equality of opportunity,—we must look to another part of the country. The typical Americanism that is represented by Lincoln owes its origin, I believe, very largely to geographical factors. It could have been developed only under certain conditions and these conditions the Middle West alone provided. The settling of the Middle West in the latter part of the eighteenth and the early part of the nineteenth centuries was part and parcel of a rigid logic of events. As Miss Semple so clearly points out in her work on the geographic conditions of American history, the Atlantic seaboard sloped toward the sea and its people held their faces eastward. They were never cut off from easy communication with the Old World, and consequently they were never quite freed from the Old World prejudices and standards. But the movement across the mountains gave rise to a new condition. The faces of the people were turned westward, and cut off from easy communication with the Old World, they developed a new set of ideals and standards under the stress of new conditions. Chief among these conditions was the immensity and richness of the territory that they were settling. The vastness of their outlook and the wealth of their resources confirmed and extended the ideals of self-reliance that they had brought with them from the seaboard. But on the seaboard, the Old World notion of social classes, the prestige of family and station, still held sway. The development of the Middle West would have been impossible under so severe a handicap. With resources so great, every stimulus must be given to individual achievement. Nothing must be permitted to stand in its way. The man who could do things, the man who could most effectively turn the forces of nature to serve the needs of society, was the man who was selected for preferment, no matter what his birth, no matter what the station of his family.

We might, in a similar fashion, review the various other ideals, which have grown out of our history, but, as I have said, my purpose is not historical but educational, and the illustrations that I have given may suffice to make my contention clear. I have attempted to show that the chief purpose of the study of history in the elementary school is to establish and fortify in the pupils' minds the significant ideals and standards of conduct which those who have gone before us have gleaned from their experience. I have maintained that, to this end, it is not only the facts of history that are important, but the appreciation of these facts. I have maintained that these prejudices and ideals have a profound influence upon conduct, and that, consequently, history is to be looked upon as a most practical branch of study.

The best way in this world to be definite is to know our goal and then strive to attain it. In the lack of definite standards based upon the lessons of the past, our dominant national ideals shift with every shifting wind of public sentiment and popular demand. Are we satisfied with the individualistic and self-centered idealism that has come with our material prosperity and which to-day shames the memory of the men who founded our Republic? Are we negligent of the serious menace that confronts any people when it loses its hold upon those goods of life that are far more precious than commercial prestige and individual aggrandizement? Are we losing our hold upon the sterner virtues which our fathers possessed,—upon the things of the spirit that are permanent and enduring?

A study of history cannot determine entirely the dominant ideals of those who pursue it. But the study of history if guided in the proper spirit and dominated by the proper aim may help. For no one who gets into the spirit of our national history,—no one who traces the origin and growth of these ideals and institutions that I have named,—can escape the conviction that the elemental virtues of courage, self-reliance, hardihood, unselfishness, self-denial, and service lie at the basis of every forward step that this country has made, and that the most precious part of our heritage is not the material comforts with which we are surrounded, but the sturdy virtues which made these comforts possible.

CHAPTER X

SCIENCE AS RELATED TO THE TEACHING OF LITERATURE[16]

The scientific method is the method of unprejudiced observation and induction. Its function in the scheme of life is to furnish man with facts and principles,—statements which mirror with accuracy and precision the conditions that may exist in any situation of any sort which man may have to face. In other words, the facts of science are important and worthy because they help us to solve the problems of life more satisfactorily. They are instrumental in their function. They are means to an end. And whenever we have a problem to solve, whenever we face a situation that demands some form of adjustment, the more accurate the information that we possess concerning this situation, the better we shall be able to solve it.

Now when I propose that we try to find out some facts about the teaching of English, and that we apply the scientific method in the discovery of these facts, I am immediately confronted with an objection. My opponent will maintain that the subject of English in our school curriculum is not one of the sciences. Taking English to mean particularly English literature rather than rhetoric or composition or grammar, it is clear that we do not teach literature as we teach the sciences. Its function differs from that of science in the curriculum. If there is a science of literature, that is not what we are teaching in the secondary schools, and that is not what most of us believe should be taught in the secondary schools. We think that the study of literature should transmit to each generation the great ideals that are crystallized in literary masterpieces. And we think that, in seeing to it that our pupils are inspired with these ideals, we should also teach literature in such a way that our pupils will be left with a desire to read good literature as a source of recreation and inspiration after they have finished the courses that we offer. When I speak of "inspiration," "appreciation," the development of "taste," and the like, I am using terms that have little direct relation to the scientific method; for, as I have said, science deals with facts, and the harder and more stubborn and more unyielding the facts become, the better they represent true science. What right have I, then, to speak of the scientific study of the teaching of English, when science and literature seem to belong to two quite separate rubrics of mental life?

I refer to this point of view, not because its inconsistencies are not fully apparent to you even upon the surface, but because it is a point of view that has hitherto

[16] A paper read before the English Section of the University of Illinois High School Conference, November 17, 1910.

interfered very materially with our educational progress. It has sometimes been assumed that, because we wish to study education scientifically, we wish to read out of it everything that cannot be reduced to a scientific formula,—that, somehow or other, we intend still further to intellectualize the processes of education and to neglect the tremendous importance of those factors that are not primarily intellectual in their nature, but which belong rather to the field of emotion and feeling.

I wish, therefore, to say at the outset that, while I firmly believe the hope of education to lie in the application of the scientific method to the solution of its problems, I still hold that neither facts nor principles nor any other products of the scientific method are the most important "goods" of life. The greatest "goods" in life are, and always must remain, I believe, its ideals, its visions, its insights, and its sympathies,—must always remain those qualities with which the teaching of literature is primarily concerned, and in the engendering of which in the hearts and souls of his pupils, the teacher of literature finds the greatest opportunity that is vouchsafed to any teacher.

The facts and principles that science has given us have been of such service to humanity that we are prone to forget that they have been of service because they have helped us more effectively to realize our ideals and attain our ends; and we are prone to forget also that, without the ideals and the ends and the visions, the facts and principles would be quite without function. I have sometimes been taken to account for separating these two factors in this way. But unless we do distinguish sharply between them, our educational thinking is bound to be hopelessly obscure.

You have all heard the story of the great chemist who was at work in his laboratory when word was brought him that his wife was dead. As the first wave of anguish swept over him, he bowed his head upon his hands and wept out his grief; but suddenly he lifted up his head, and held before him his hands wet with tears. "Tears!" he cried; "what are they? I have analyzed them: a little chloride of sodium, some alkaline salts, a little mucin, and some water. That is all." And he went back to his work.

The story is an old one, and very likely apocryphal, but it is not without its lesson to us in the present connection. Unless we distinguish between these two factors that I have named, we are likely either to take this man's attitude or something approaching it, or to go to the other extreme, renounce the accuracy and precision of the scientific method, and give ourselves up to the cult of emotionalism.

Now, while we do not wish to read out of the teaching of literature the factors of appreciation and inspiration, we do wish to find out how these important functions of our teaching may be best fulfilled. And it is here that facts and principles gained by the scientific method not only can but must furnish the ultimate solution. We have a problem. That problem, it is true, is concerned with something that is not scientific, and to attempt to make it scientific is to kill the very life that it is our problem to cherish. But in solving that problem, we must take certain steps; we must arrange our materials in certain ways; we must adjust hard and stubborn facts to the attainment of our end. What are these facts? What is their relation to our problem? What laws govern their operation? These are subordinate but very essential parts of our larger problem, and it is through the scientific investigation of these subordinate problems that our larger problem is to be solved.

Let me give you an illustration of what I mean. We may assume that every boy who goes out of the high school should appreciate the meaning and worth of self-sacrifice as this is revealed (not expounded) in Dickens's delineation of the character of Sidney Carton. There is our problem,—but what a host of subordinate problems at once confront us! Where shall we introduce *The Tale of Two Cities*? Will it be in the second year, or the third, or the fourth? Will it be best preceded by the course in general history which will give the pupil a time perspective upon the crimson background of the French Revolution against which Dickens projected his master character? Or shall we put *The Tale of Two Cities* first for the sake of the heightened interest which the art of the novelist may lend to the facts of the historian? Again, how may the story be best presented? What part shall the pupils read in class? What part shall they read at home? What part, if any, shall we read to them? What questions are necessary to insure appreciation? How many of the allusions need be run down in order to give the maximal effect of the masterpiece? How may the necessarily discontinuous discussions of the class—one period each day for several days—be so counteracted as to insure the cumulative emotional effect which the appreciation of all art presupposes? Should the story be sketched through first, and then read in some detail, or will one reading suffice?

These are problems, I repeat, that stand to the chief problem as means stand to end. Now some of these questions must be solved by every teacher for himself, but that does not prevent each teacher from solving them scientifically. Others, it is clear, might be solved once and for all by the right kind of an investigation,—might result in permanent and universal laws which any one could apply.

There are, of course, several ways in which answers for these questions may be secured. One way is that of *a priori* reasoning,—the deductive procedure. This method may be thoroughly scientific, depending of course upon the validity of our general principles as applied to the specific problem. Ordinarily this validity can be determined only by trial; consequently these *a priori* inferences should be looked upon as hypotheses to be tested by trial under standard conditions. For example, I might argue that *The Tale of Two Cities* should be placed in the third year because the emotional ferment of adolescence is then most favorable for the engendering of the ideal. But in the first place, this assumed principle would itself be subject to grave question and it would also have to be determined whether there is so little variation among the pupils in respect of physiological age as to permit the application to all of a generalization that might conceivably apply only to the average child. In other words, all of our generalizations applying to average pupils must be applied with a knowledge of the extent and range of variation from the average. Some people say that there is no such thing as an average child, but, for all practical purposes, the average child is a very real reality,—he is, in fact, more numerous than any other single class; but this does not mean that there may be not enough variations from the average to make unwise the application of our principle.

I refer to this hypothetical case to show the extreme difficulty of reaching anything more than hypotheses by *a priori* reasoning. We have a certain number of fairly well established general principles in secondary education. Perhaps those most frequently employed are our generalizations regarding adolescence and its influences upon the mental and especially the emotional life of high-school pupils. Stanley Hall's work in this field is wonderfully stimulating and suggestive, and yet we should not forget that most of his generalizations are, after all, only plausible hypotheses to be acted upon as tentative guides for practice and to be tested carefully under controlled conditions, rather than to be accepted as immutable and unchangeable laws. We sometimes assume that all high-school pupils are adolescents, when the likelihood is that an appreciable proportion of pupils in the first two years have not yet reached this important node of their development.

I say this not to minimize in any way the importance that attaches to adolescent characteristics, but rather to suggest that you who are daily dealing with these pupils can in the aggregate add immeasurably to the knowledge that we now have concerning this period. A tremendous waste is constantly going on in that most precious of all our possible resources,—namely, human experience. How many problems that are well solved have to be solved again and again because the experience has not been crystallized in a well-tested fact or principle; how many experiences that might be well worth the effort that they cost are quite worthless because, in undergoing them, we have neglected some one or another of the rules that govern inexorably the validity of our inferences and conclusions. That is all that the scientific method means in the last analysis: it is a system of principles that enable us to make our experience worth while in meeting later situations. We all have the opportunity of contributing to the sum total of human knowledge, if only we know the rules of the game.

I said that one way of solving these subordinate problems that arise in the realization of our chief aims in teaching is the *a priori* method of applying general principles to the problems. Another method is to imitate the way in which we have seen some one else handle the situation. Now this may be the most effective way possible. In fact, if a sufficient number of generations of teachers keep on blindly plunging in and floundering about in solving their problems, the most effective methods will ultimately be evolved through what we call the process of trial and error. The teaching of the very oldest subjects in the curriculum is almost always the best and most effective teaching, for the very reason that the blundering process has at last resulted in an effective procedure. But the scientific method of solving problems has its very function in preventing the tremendous waste that this process involves. English literature is a comparatively recent addition to the secondary curriculum. Its possibilities of service are almost unlimited. Shall we wait for ten or fifteen generations of teachers to blunder out the most effective means of teaching it, or shall we avail ourselves of these simple principles which will enable us to concentrate this experience within one or two generations?

I should like to emphasize one further point. No one has greater respect than I have for what we term experience in teaching. But let me say that a great deal of what we may term "crude" experience—that is, experience that has not been refined by the application of scientific method—is most untrustworthy,—unless, indeed, it has been garnered and winnowed and sifted through the ages. Let me give you an example of some accepted dictums of educational experience that controlled investigations have shown to be untrustworthy.

It is a general impression among teachers that specific habits may be generalized; that habits of neatness and accuracy developed in one line of work, for example, will inevitably make one neater and more accurate in other things. It has been definitely proved that this transfer of training does not take place inevitably, but in reality demands the fulfillment of certain conditions of which education has become fully conscious only within a comparatively short time, and as a result of careful, systematic, controlled experimentation. The meaning of this in the prevention of waste through inadequate teaching is fully apparent.

Again, it has been supposed by many teachers that the home environment is a large factor in the success or failure of a pupil in school. In every accurate and controlled investigation that has been conducted so far it has been shown that this factor in such subjects as arithmetic and spelling at least is so small as to be absolutely negligible in practice.

Some people still believe that a teacher is born and not made, and yet a careful investigation of the efficiency of elementary teachers shows that, when such teachers were ranked by competent judges, specialized training stood out as the most important factor in general efficiency. In this same investigation, the time-honored notion that a college education will, irrespective of specialized training, adequately equip a teacher for his work was revealed as a fallacy,—for twenty-eight per cent of the normal-school graduates among all the teachers were in the first and second ranks of efficiency as against only seventeen per cent of the college graduates; while, in the two lowest ranks, only sixteen per cent of the normal-school graduates are to be found as against forty-four per cent of the college graduates. These investigations, I may add, were made by university professors, and I am giving them here in a university classroom and as a university representative. And of course I shall hasten to add that general scholarship is one important essential. Our mistake has been in assuming sometimes that it is the only essential.

Very frequently the controlled experience of scientific investigation confirms a principle that has been derived from crude experience. Most teachers will agree, for example, that a certain amount of drill and repetition is absolutely essential in the mastery of any subject. Every time that scientific investigation has touched this problem it has unmistakably confirmed this belief. Some very recent investigations made by Mr. Brown at the Charleston Normal School show conclusively that five-minute drill periods preceding every lesson in arithmetic place pupils who undergo such periods far in advance of others who spend this time in non-drill arithmetical work, and that this improvement holds not only in the number habits, but also in the reasoning processes.

Other similar cases could be cited, but I have probably said enough to make my point, and my point is this: that crude experience is an unsafe guide for practice; that experience may be refined in two ways—first by the slow, halting, wasteful operation of time, which has established many principles upon a pinnacle of security from which they will never be shaken, but which has also accomplished this result at the cost of innumerable mistakes, blunders, errors, futile efforts, and heartbreaking failures; or secondly, by the application of the principles of control and test which are now at our service, and which permit present-day teachers to concentrate within a single generation the growth and development and progress that the empirical method of trial and error could not encompass in a millennium.

The teaching of English merits treatment by this method. I recommend strongly that you give the plan a trial. You may not get immediate results. You may not get valuable results. But in any case, if you carefully respect the scientific proprieties, your experience will be worth vastly more than ten times the amount of crude experience; and, whether you get results or not, you will undergo a valuable discipline from which may emerge the ideals of science if you are not already imbued with them. I always tell my students that, even in the study of science itself, it is the ideals of science,—the ideals of patient, thoughtful work, the ideals of open-mindedness and caution in reaching conclusions, the ideals of unprejudiced observation from which selfishness and personal desire are eliminated,—it is these ideals that are vastly more important than the facts of science as such,—and these latter are significant enough to have made possible our present progress and our present amenities of life.

CHAPTER XI

THE NEW ATTITUDE TOWARD DRILL[17]

Wandering about in a circle through a thick forest is perhaps an overdrawn analogy to our activity in attempting to construct educational theories; and yet there is a resemblance. We push out hopefully—and often boastfully—into the unknown wilderness, absolutely certain that we are pioneering a trail that will later become the royal highway to learning. We struggle on, ruthlessly using the hatchet and the ax to clear the road before us. And all too often we come back to our starting point, having unwittingly described a perfect circle, instead of the straight line that we had anticipated.

But I am not a pessimist, and I like to believe that, although our course frequently resembles a circle, it is much better to characterize it as a spiral, and that, although we do get back to a point that we recognize, it is not, after all, our old starting point; it is an homologous point on a higher plane. We have at least climbed a little, even if we have not traveled in a straight line.

Now in a figurative way this explains how we have come to take our present attitude toward the problem of drill or training in the process of education. Drill means the repetition of a process until it has become mechanical or automatic. It means the kind of discipline that the recruit undergoes in the army,—the making of a series of complicated movements so thoroughly automatic that they will be gone through with accurately and precisely, at the word of command. It means the sort of discipline that makes certain activities machine-like in their operation,—so that we do not have to think about which one comes next. Thus the mind is relieved of the burden of looking after the innumerable details and may use its precious energy for a more important purpose.

In every adult life, a large number of these mechanized responses are absolutely essential to efficiency. Modern civilized life is so highly organized that it demands a multitude of reactions and adjustments which primitive life did not demand. It goes without saying that there are innumerable little details of our daily work that must be reduced to the plane of unvarying habit. These details vary with the trade or profession of the individual; hence general education cannot hope to supply the individual with all of the automatic responses that he will need. But, in addition to these specialized responses, there is a large mass of responses that are common to every member of the social group. We must all be able to communicate with one another, both through the medium of speech, and through the medium

[17] An address before the Kansas State Teachers' Association, Topeka, October 20, 1910.

of written and printed symbols. We live in a society that is founded upon the principle of the division of labor. We must exchange the products of our labor for the necessities of life that we do not ourselves produce, and hence arises the necessity for the short cuts to counting and measurement which we call arithmetic. And finally we must all live together in something at least approaching harmony; hence the thousand and one little responses that mean courtesy and good manners must be made thoroughly automatic.

Now education, from the very earliest times, has recognized the necessity of building up these automatic responses,—of fixing these essential habits in all individuals. This recognition has often been short-sighted and sometimes even blind; but it has served to hold education rather tenaciously to a process that all must admit to be essential.

Drill or training, however, is unfortunate in one important particular. It invariably involves repetition; and conscious, explicit repetition tends to become monotonous. We must hold attention to the drill process, and yet attention abhors monotony as nature abhors a vacuum. Consequently no small part of the tedium and irksomeness of school work has been due to its emphasis of drill. The formalism of the older schools has been described, criticized, and lampooned in professional literature, and even in the pages of fiction. The disastrous results that follow from engendering in pupils a disgust for school and all that it represents have been eloquently portrayed. Along with the tendency toward ease and comfort in other departments of human life has gone a parallel tendency to relieve the school of this odious burden of formal, lifeless, repetitive work.

This "reform movement," as I shall call it, represents our first plunge into the wilderness. We would get away from the entanglements of drill and into the clearings of pleasurable, spontaneous activities. A new sun of hope dawned upon the educational world.

You are all familiar with some of the more spectacular results of this movement. You have heard of the schools that eliminated drill processes altogether, and depended upon clear initial development to fix the facts and formulæ and reactions that every one needs. You have heard and perhaps seen some of the schools that were based entirely upon the doctrine of spontaneity, governing their work by the principle that the child should never do anything that he did not wish to do at the moment of doing,—although the advocates of this theory generally qualified their principle by insisting that the skillful teacher would have the child wish to do the right thing all the time.

Let me describe to you a school of this type that I once visited. I learned of it through a resident of the city in which it was located. He was delivering an address before an educational gathering on the problems of modern education. He told the audience that, in the schools of this enlightened city, the antiquated notions that were so pernicious had been entirely dispensed with. He said that pupils in these schools were no longer repressed; that all regimentation, line passing, static posture, and other barbaric practices had been abolished; that the pupils were free to work out their own destiny, to realize themselves, through all forms of constructive activity; that drills had been eliminated; that corporal punishment was never even mentioned, much less practiced; that all was harmony, and love, and freedom, and spontaneity.

I listened to this speaker with intense interest, and, as his picture unfolded, I became more and more convinced that this city had at last solved the problem. I took the earliest opportunity to visit its schools. When I reached the city I went to the superintendent's office. I asked to be directed to the best school. "Our schools are all 'best,'" the secretary told me with an intonation that denoted commendable pride, and which certainly made me feel extremely humble, for here even the laws of logic and of formal grammar had been transcended. I made bold to apologize, however, and amended my request to make it apparent that I wished to see the largest school. I was directed to take a certain car and, in due time, found myself at the school. I inferred that recess was in progress when I reached the building, and that the recess was being celebrated within doors. After some time spent in dodging about the corridors, I at last located the principal.

I introduced myself and asked if I could visit his school after recess was over. "We have no recesses here," he replied (I could just catch his voice above the din of the corridors); "this is a relaxation period for some of the classes." He led the way to the office, and I spent a few moments in getting the "lay of the land." I asked him, first, whether he agreed with the doctrines that the system represented, and he told me that he believed in them implicitly. Did he follow them out consistently in the operation of his school? Yes, he followed them out to the letter.

We then went to several classrooms, where I saw children realizing themselves, I thought, very effectively. There were three groups at work in each room. One recited to the teacher, another studied at the seats, a third did construction work at the tables. I inquired about the mechanics of this rather elaborate organization, but I was told that mechanics had been eliminated from this school. Mechanical organization of the classroom, it seems, crushes the child's spontaneity, represses his self-activity, prevents the effective operation of the principle of self-realization. How, then, did these three groups exchange places, for I felt that the doctrine of self-realization would not permit them to remain in the same employment during the entire session. "Oh," the principal replied, "when they get ready to change, they change, that's all."

I saw that a change was coming directly, so I waited to watch it. The group had been working with what I should call a great deal of noise and confusion. All at once this increased tenfold. Pupils jumped over seats, ran into each other in the aisles, scurried and scampered from this place to that, while the teacher stood in the front of the room wildly waving her arms. The performance lasted several minutes. "There's spontaneity for you," the principal shouted above the roar of the storm. I acquiesced by a nod of the head,—my lungs, through lack of training, being unequal to the emergency.

We passed to another room. The same group system was in evidence. I noticed pupils who had been working at their seats suddenly put away their books and papers and skip over to the construction table. I asked concerning the nature of the construction work. "We use it," the principal told me, "as a reward for good work in the book subjects. You see arithmetic is dead and dry. You must give pupils an incentive to master it. We make the privileges of the construction table the incentive." "What do they make at this table?" I asked. "Whatever their fancy dictates," he replied. I was a little curious, however, to know how it all come out. I saw one child start to work on a basket, work at it a few minutes, then take up something else, continue a little time, go back to the basket, and finally throw both down for a third object of self-realization. I called the principal's attention to this phenomenon. "How do you get the beautiful results that you exhibit?" I asked. "For those," he said, "we just keep the pupils working on one thing until it is finished." "But," I objected, "is that consistent with the doctrine of spontaneity?" His answer was lost in the din of a change of groups, and I did not follow the investigation further.

Noon dismissal was due when I went into the corridor. Lines are forbidden in that school. At the stroke of the bell, the classroom doors burst open and bedlam was let loose. I had anticipated what was coming, and hurriedly betook myself to an alcove. I saw more spontaneity in two minutes than I had ever seen before in my life. Some boys tore through the corridors at breakneck speed and down the stairways, three steps at a time. Others sauntered along, realizing various propensities by pushing and shoving each other, snatching caps out of others' hands, slapping each other over the head with books, and various other expressions of exuberant spirits. One group stopped in front of my alcove, and showed commendable curiosity about the visitor in their midst. After exhausting his static possibilities, they tempted him to dynamic reaction by making faces; but this proving to be of no avail, they went on their way,—in the hope, doubtless, of realizing themselves elsewhere.

I left that school with a fairly firm conviction that I had seen the most advanced notions of educational theory worked out to a logical conclusion. There was nothing halfway about it. There was no apology offered for anything that happened. It was all fair and square and open and aboveboard. To be sure, the pupils were, to my prejudiced mind, in a condition approaching anarchy, but I could not deny the spontaneity, nor could I deny self-activity, nor could I deny self-realization. These principles were evidently operating without let or hindrance.

Before leaving the school, I took occasion to inquire concerning the effect of such a system upon the teachers. I led up to it by asking the principal if there were any nervous or anæmic children in his school. "Not one," he replied enthusiastically; "our system eliminates them." "But how about the teachers?" I ventured to remark, having in mind the image of a distracted young woman whom I had seen attempting to reduce forty little ruffians to some semblance of law and order through moral suasion. If I judged conditions correctly, that woman was on the verge of a nervous breakdown. My guide became confidential when I made this inquiry. "To tell the truth," he whispered, "the system is mighty hard on the women."

A few years ago I had the privilege of visiting a high school which was operated upon this same principle. I visited in that school some classes that were taught by men and women, whom I should number among the most expert teachers that I have ever seen. The instruction that these men and women were giving was as clear and lucid as one could desire. And yet, in spite of that excellent instruction, pupils read newspapers, prepared other lessons, or read books during the recitations, and did all this openly and unreproved. They responded to their instructors with shameless insolence. Young ladies of sixteen and seventeen coming from cultured homes were permitted in this school to pull each other's hair, pinch the arms of schoolmates who were reciting, and behave themselves in general as if they were savages. The pupils lolled in their seats, passed notes, kept up an undertone of conversation, arose from their seats at the first tap of the bell, and piled in disorder out of the classroom while the instructor was still talking. If the lessons had been tedious, one might perhaps at least have palliated such conduct, but the instruction was very far from tedious. It was bright, lively, animated, beautifully clear, and admirably illustrated. It is simply the theory of this school never to interfere with the spontaneous activity of the pupils. And I may add that the school draws its enrollment very largely from wealthy families who believe that their children are being given the best that modern education has developed, that they are not being subjected to the deadening methods of the average public school, and above all that their manners are not being corrupted by promiscuous mingling with the offspring of illiterate immigrants. And yet soon afterward, I visited a high school in one of the poorest slum districts of a large city. I saw pupils well-behaved, courteous to one another, to their instructors, and to visitors. The instruction was much below that given in the first school in point of quality, and yet the pupils were getting from it, even under these conditions, vastly more than were the pupils of the other school from their masterly instructors.

The two schools that I first described represent one type of the attempt that education has made to pioneer a new path through the wilderness. I have said that many of these attempts have ended by bringing the adventurers back to their starting point. I cannot say so much for these schools. The movement that they represent is still floundering about in the tamarack swamps, getting farther and farther into the morass, with little hope of ever emerging.

May I tax your patience with one more concrete illustration: this time, of a school that seems to me to have reached the starting point, but on that new and higher plane of which I have spoken?

This school is in a small Massachusetts town, and is the model department of the state normal school located at that place. The first point that impressed me was typified by a boy of about twelve who was passing through the corridor as I entered the building. Instead of slouching along, wasting every possible moment before he should return to his room, he was walking briskly as if eager to get back to his work. Instead of staring at the stranger within his gates with the impudent curiosity so often noticed in children of this age, he greeted me pleasantly and wished to know if I were looking for the principal. When I told him that I was, he informed me that the principal was on the upper floor, but that he would go for him at once. He did, and returned a moment later saying that the head of the school would be down directly, and asked me to wait in the office, into which he ushered me with all the courtesy of a private secretary. Then he excused himself and went directly to his room.

Now that might have been an exceptional case, but I found out later that is was not. Wherever I went in that school, the pupils were polite and courteous and respectful. That was part of their education. It should be part of every child's education. But many schools are too busy teaching reading, writing, and arithmetic, and others are too busy preserving discipline, and others are too busy coquetting for the good will of their pupils and trying to amuse them—too busy to give heed to a set of habits that are of paramount importance in the life of civilized society. This school took up the matter of training in good manners as an essential part of its duty, and it accomplished this task quickly and effectively. It did it by utilizing the opportunities presented in the usual course of school work. It took a little time and a little attention, for good manners cannot be acquired incidentally any more than the multiplication tables can be acquired incidentally; but it utilized the everyday opportunities of the schoolroom, and did not make morals and manners the subject of instruction for a half-hour on Friday afternoons to be completely forgotten during the rest of the week.

When the principal took me through the school, I noted everywhere a happy and courteous relation between pupils and teachers. They spoke pleasantly to one another. I heard no nagging or scolding. I saw no one sulking or pouting or in bad temper. And yet there was every evidence of respect and obedience on the part of the pupils. There was none of that happy-go-lucky comradeship which I have sometimes seen in other modern schools, and which leads the pupil to understand that his teacher is there to gain his interest, not to command his respectful attention. Pupils were too busy with their work to talk much with one another. They were sitting up in their seats as a matter of habit, and it did not seem to hurt them seriously to do so. And everywhere they were working like beavers at one task or another, or attending with all their eyes and ears to a recitation.

Now it seemed to me that this school was operated with a minimum of waste or loss. Every item of energy that the pupils possessed was being given to some educative activity. Nothing was lost by conflict between pupil and teacher. Nothing was lost by bursts of anger or by fits of depression. These sources of waste had been eliminated so far as I could determine. The pupils could read well and write well and cipher accurately. They even took a keen delight in the drills. And I found that this phase of their work was enlightened by the modern content that had been introduced. In their handwork and manual training they could see that arithmetic was useful,—that it had something to do with the great big buzzing life of the outer world. They learned that spelling was useful in writing,—that it was not something that began and ended within the covers of the spelling book, but that it had a real and vital relation to other things that they found to be important. They had their dramatic exercises in which they and their fellows, and, on occasions, their parents, took a keen delight, and they were glad to afford them pleasure and to receive congratulations at the close. And yet they found that, in order to do these things well, they must read and study and drill on speaking. They liked to have their drawings inspected and praised at the school exhibitions, but they soon found that good drawing and painting and designing were strictly conditioned by a mastery of technique, and they wished to master technique in order to win these rewards.

Now what was the secret of the efficiency of this school? Not merely the fact that it had introduced certain types of content such as drawing, manual training, domestic science, dramatization, story work,—but also that it had not lost sight of the fundamental purpose of elementary education, but had so organized all of its studies that each played into the hands of the others, and that everything that was done had some definite and tangible relation to everything else. The manual training exercises and the mechanical drawing were exercises in arithmetic, but, let me remind you, there were other lessons, and formal lessons, in arithmetic as well. But the one exercise enlightened and made more meaningful the other. In the same way the story and dramatization were intimately related to the reading and the language, but there were formal lessons in reading and formal lessons in language. The geography illustrated nature study and employed language and arithmetic and drawing in its exercises. And so the whole structure was organized and coherent and unified, and what was taught in one class was utilized in another. There was no needless duplication, no needless or meaningless repetition. But repetition there was, over and over again, but always it was effective in still more firmly fixing the habits.

One would be an ingrate, indeed, if one failed to recognize the great good that an extreme reform movement may do. Some very precious increments of progress have resulted even from the most extreme and ridiculous reactions against the drill and formalism of the older schools. Let me briefly summarize these really substantial gains as I conceive them.

In the first place, we have come to recognize distinctly the importance of enlisting in the service of habit building the native instincts of the child. Up to a certain point nature provides for the fixing of useful responses, and we should be unwise not to make use of these tendencies. In the spontaneous activities of play, certain fundamental reactions are continually repeated until they reach the plane of absolute mechanism. In imitating the actions of others, adjustments are learned and made into habits without effort; in fact, the process of imitation, so far as it is instinctive, is a source of pure delight to the young child. Finally, closely related to these two instincts, is the native tendency to repetition,—nature's primary provision for drill. You have often heard little children repeat their new words over and over again. Frequently they have no conception of the meanings of these words. Nature seems to be untroubled by a question that has bothered teachers; namely, Should a child ever be asked to drill on something the purpose of which he does not understand? Nature sees to it that certain essential responses become automatic long before the child is conscious of their meaning. Just because nature does this is, of course, no reason why we should imitate her. But the fact is an interesting commentary upon the extreme to which we sometimes carry our principle of rationalizing everything before permitting it to be mastered.

I repeat that the reform movement has done excellent service in extending the recognition in education of these fundamental and inborn adaptive instincts,—play, imitation, and rhythmic repetition. It has erred when it has insisted that we could depend upon these alone, for nature has adapted man, not to the complicated conditions of our modern highly organized social life, but rather to primitive conditions. Left to themselves, these instinctive forces would take the child up to a certain point, but they would still leave him on a primitive plane. I know of one good authority on the teaching of reading who maintains that the normal child would learn to read without formal teaching if he were placed in the right environment,—an environment of books. This may be possible with some exceptional children, but even an environment reasonably replete with books does not effect this miracle in the case of certain children whom I know very well and whom I like to think of as perfectly normal. These children learned to talk by imitation and instinctive repetition. But nature has not yet gone so far as to provide the average child with spontaneous impulses that will lead him to learn to read. Reading is a much more complicated and highly organized process. And so it is with a vast number of the activities that our pupils must master.

Another increment of progress that the reform movement has given to educational practice is a recognition of the fact that we have been requiring pupils to acquire unnecessary habits, under the impression, that even if the habits were not useful, something of value was gained in their acquisition. As a result, we have passed all of our grain through the same mill, unmindful of the fact that different life activities required different types of grist. To-day we are seeing the need for carefully selecting the types of habit and skill that should be developed in *all* children. We are recognizing that there are many phases of the educative process that it is not well to reduce to an automatic basis. When I was in the elementary school I memorized Barnes's *History of the United States* and Harper's *Geography* from cover to cover. I have never greatly regretted this automatic mastery; but I have often thought that I might have memorized something rather more important, for history and geography could have been mastered just as effectively in another way.

In the third place, and most important of all, we have been led to analyze this complex process of habit building,—to find out the factors that operate in learning. We have now a goodly body of principles that may even be characterized by the adjective "scientific." We know that in habit building, it is fundamentally essential to get the pupil started in the right way. A recent writer states that two thirds of the difficulty that the teacher meets fixing habits is due to the neglect of this principle. Inadequate and inefficient habits get started and must be continually combated while the desirable habit is being formed. How important this is in the initial presentation of material that is to be memorized or made automatic we are just now beginning to appreciate. One writer insists that faulty work in the first grade is responsible for a large part of the retardation which is bothering us so much today. The wrong kind of a start is made, and whenever a faulty habit is formed, it much more than doubles the difficulty of getting the right one well under way. We are slowly coming to appreciate how much time is wasted in drill processes by inadequate methods. Technique is being improved and the time thus saved is being given to the newer content subjects that are demanding admission to the schools.

Again, we are coming to appreciate as never before the importance of motivating our drill work,—of not only reading into it purpose and meaning so that the pupil will understand what it is all for, but also of engendering in him the *desire* to form the habits,—to undergo the discipline that is essential for mastery. Here again the reform movement has been helpful, showing us the waste of time and energy that results from attempting to fix habits that are only weakly motivated.

All this is a vastly different matter from sugar-coating the drill processes, under the mistaken notion that something that is worth while may be acquired without effort. I think that educators are generally agreed that such a policy is thoroughly bad,—for it subverts a basic principle of human life the operation of which neither education nor any other force can alter or reverse. To teach the child that the things in life that are worth doing are easy to do, or that they are always or even often intrinsically pleasant or agreeable, is to teach him a lie. Human history gives us no examples of worthy achievements that have not been made at the price of struggle and effort,—at the price of doing things that men did not want to do. Every great truth has had to struggle upward from defeat. Every man who has really found himself in the work of life has paid the price of sacrifice for his success. And whenever we attempt to give our pupils a mastery of the complicated arts and skills that have lifted civilized man above the plane of his savage ancestors, we must expect from them struggle and effort and self-denial.

Let me quote a paragraph from the report of a recent investigation in the psychology of learning. The habit that was being learned in this experiment was skill in the use of the typewriter. The writer describes the process in the following words:

> "In the early stages of learning, our subjects were all very much interested in the work. Their whole mind seemed to be spontaneously held by the writing. They were always anxious to take up the work anew each day. Their general attitude and the resultant sensations constituted a pleasant feeling tone, which had a helpful reactionary effect upon the work. Continued practice, however, brought a change. In place of the spontaneous, rapt attention of the beginning stages, attention tended, at certain definite stages of advancement, to wander away from the work. A general feeling of monotony, which at times assumed the form of utter disgust, took the place of the former pleasant sensations and feelings. The writing became a disagreeable task. The unpleasant feelings now present in consciousness exerted an ever-restraining effect on the work. As an expert skill was approached, however, the learners' attitude and mood changed again. They again took a keen interest in the work. Their whole feeling tone once more became favorable, and the movements delightful and pleasant. The expert typist . . . so thoroughly enjoyed the writing that it was as pleasant as the spontaneous play activities of a child. But in the course of developing this permanent interest in the work, there were many periods in nearly every test, many days, as well as stages in the practice as a whole, when the work was much disliked, periods when the learning assumed the rôle of a very

> monotonous task. Our records showed that at such times as these no progress was made. Rapid progress in learning typewriting was made only when the learners were feeling good and had an attitude of interest toward the work."[18]

Who has not experienced that feeling of hopelessness and despair that comes at these successive levels of the long process of acquiring skill in a complicated art? How desperately we struggle on—striving to put every item of energy that we can command into our work, and yet feeling how hopeless it all seems. How tempting then is the hammock on the porch, the fascinating novel that we have placed on our bedside table, the happy company of friends that are talking and laughing in the next room; or how we long for the green fields and the open road; how seductive is that siren call of change and diversion,—that evil spirit of procrastination! How feeble, too, are the efforts that we make under these conditions! We are not making progress in our art, we are only marking time. And yet the psychologists tell us that this marking time is an essential in the mastery of any complicated art. Somewhere, deep down in the nervous system, subtle processes are at work, and when finally interest dawns,—when finally hope returns to us, and life again becomes worth while,—these heartbreaking struggles reap their reward. The psychologists call them "plateaus of growth," but some one has said that "sloughs of despond" would be a far better designation.

The progress of any individual depends upon his ability to pass through these sloughs of despond,—to set his face resolutely to the task and persevere. It would be the idlest folly to lead children to believe that success or achievement or even passing ability can be gained in any other manner. And this is the danger in the sugar-coating process.

But motivation does not mean sugar-coating. It means the development of purpose, of ambition, of incentive. It means the development of the willingness to undergo the discipline in order that the purpose may be realized, in order that the goal may be attained. It means the creating of those conditions that make for strength and virility and moral fiber,—for it is in the consciousness of having overcome obstacles and won in spite of handicaps,—it is in this consciousness of conquest that mental strength and moral strength have their source. The victory that really strengthens one is not the victory that has come easily, but the victory that stands out sharp and clear against the background of effort and struggle. It is because this subjective contrast is so absolutely essential to the consciousness of power,—it is for this reason that the "sloughs of despond" still have their function in our new attitude toward drill.

But do not mistake me: I have no sympathy with that educational "stand-pattism" that would multiply these needlessly, or fail to build solid and comfortable highways across them wherever it is possible to do so. I have no sympathy with that philosophy of education which approves the placing of artificial barriers in the learner's path. But if I build highways across the morasses, it is only that youth may the more readily traverse the region and come the more quickly to the points where struggle is absolutely necessary.

[18] W.F. Book, *Journal of Educational Psychology*, vol. i, 1910, p. 195.

You remember in George Eliot's *Daniel Deronda* the story of Gwendolen Harleth. Gwendolen was a butterfly of society, a young woman in whose childhood drill and discipline had found no place. In early womanhood, she was, through family misfortune, thrown upon her own resources. In casting about for some means of self-support her first recourse was to music, for which she had some taste and in which she had had some slight training. She sought out her old German music teacher, Klesmer, and asked him what she might do to turn this taste and this training to financial account. Klesmer's reply sums up in a nutshell the psychology of skill:

> "Any great achievement in acting or in music grows with the growth. Whenever an artist has been able to say, 'I came, I saw, I conquered,' it has been at the end of patient practice. Genius, at first, is little more than a great capacity for receiving discipline. Singing and acting, like the fine dexterity of the juggler with his cup and balls, require a shaping of the organs toward a finer and finer certainty of effect. Your muscles, your whole frame, must go like a watch,—true, true, true, to a hair. This is the work of the springtime of life before the habits have been formed."

And I can formulate my own conception of the work of habit building in education no better than by paraphrasing Klesmer's epigram. To increase in our pupils the capacity to receive discipline; to show them, through concrete example, over and over again, how persistence and effort and concentration bring results that are worth while; to choose from their own childish experiences the illustrations that will force this lesson home; to supplement, from the stories of great achievements, those illustrations which will inspire them to effort; to lead them to see that Peary conquering the Pole, or Wilbur Wright perfecting the aëroplane, or Morse struggling through long years of hopelessness and discouragement to give the world the electric telegraph,—to show them that these men went through experiences differing only in degree and not in kind from those which characterize every achievement, no matter how small, so long as it is dominated by a unitary purpose; to make the inevitable sloughs of despond no less morasses, perhaps, but to make their conquest add a permanent increment to growth and development: this is the task of our drill work as I view it. As the prophecy of Isaiah has it: "Precept must be upon precept; precept upon precept; line upon line; line upon line; here a little and there a little." And if we can succeed in giving our pupils this vision,—if we can reveal the deeper meaning of struggle and effort and self-denial and sacrifice shining out through the little details of the day's work,—we are ourselves achieving something that is richly worth while; for the highest triumph of the teacher's art is to get his pupils to see, in the small and seemingly trivial affairs of everyday life, the operation of fundamental and eternal principles.

CHAPTER XII

THE IDEAL TEACHER[19]

I wish to discuss with you briefly a very commonplace and oft-repeated theme,—a theme that has been handled and handled until its once-glorious raiment is now quite threadbare; a theme so full of pitfalls and dangers for one who would attempt its discussion that I have hesitated long before making a choice. I know of no other theme that lends itself so readily to a superficial treatment—of no theme upon which one could find so easily at hand all of the proverbs and platitudes and maxims that one might desire. And so I cannot be expected to say anything upon this topic that has not been said before in a far better manner. But, after all, very few of our thoughts—even of those that we consider to be the most original and worth while—are really new to the world. Most of our thoughts have been thought before. They are like dolls that are passed on from age to age to be dressed up and decorated to suit the taste or the fashion or the fancy of each succeeding generation. But even a new dress may add a touch of newness to an old doll; and a new phrase or a new setting may, for a moment, rejuvenate an old truth.

The topic that I wish to treat is this, "The Ideal Teacher." And I may as well start out by saying that the ideal teacher is and always must be a figment of the imagination. This is the essential feature of any ideal. The ideal man, for example, must possess an infinite number of superlative characteristics. We take this virtue from one, and that from another, and so on indefinitely until we have constructed in imagination a paragon, the counterpart of which could never exist on earth. He would have all the virtues of all the heroes; but he would lack all their defects and all their inadequacies. He would have the manners of a Chesterfield, the courage of a Winkelried, the imagination of a Dante, the eloquence of a Cicero, the wit of a Voltaire, the intuitions of a Shakespeare, the magnetism of a Napoleon, the patriotism of a Washington, the loyalty of a Bismarck, the humanity of a Lincoln, and a hundred other qualities, each the counterpart of some superlative quality, drawn from the historic figure that represented that quality in richest measure.

And so it is with the ideal teacher: he would combine, in the right proportion, all of the good qualities of all of the good teachers that we have ever known or heard of. The ideal teacher is and always must be a creature, not of flesh and blood, but of the imagination, a child of the brain. And perhaps it is well that this is true; for, if he existed in the flesh, it would not take very many of him to put the rest of us out of business. The relentless law of compensation, which rules that unusual

[19] An address to the graduating class of the Oswego, New York, State Normal School, February, 1908.

growth in one direction must always be counterbalanced by deficient growth in another direction, is the saving principle of human society. That a man should be superlatively good in one single line of effort is the demand of modern life. It is a platitude to say that this is the age of the specialist. But specialism, while it always means a gain to society, also always means a loss to the individual. Darwin, at the age of forty, suddenly awoke to the fact that he was a man of one idea. Twenty years before, he had been a youth of the most varied and diverse interests. He had enjoyed music, he had found delight in the masterpieces of imaginative literature, he had felt a keen interest in the drama, in poetry, in the fine arts. But at forty Darwin quite by accident discovered that these things had not attracted him for years,—that every increment of his time and energy was concentrated in a constantly increasing measure upon the unraveling of that great problem to which he had set himself. And he lamented bitterly the loss of these other interests; he wondered why he had been so thoughtless as to let them slip from his grasp. It was the same old story of human progress; the sacrifice of the individual to the race. For Darwin's loss was the world's gain, and if he had not limited himself to one line of effort, and given himself up to that work to the exclusion of everything else, the world might still be waiting for the *Origin of Species*, and the revolution in human thought and human life which followed in the wake of that great book. Carlyle defined genius as an infinite capacity for taking pains. George Eliot characterized it as an infinite capacity for receiving discipline. But to make the definition complete, we need the formulation of Goethe, who identified genius with the power of concentration: "Who would be great must limit his ambitions; in concentration is shown the Master."

And so the great men of history, from the very fact of their genius, are apt not to correspond with what our ideal of greatness demands. Indeed, our ideal is often more nearly realized in men who fall far short of genius. When I studied chemistry, the instructor burned a bit of diamond to prove to us that the diamond was, after all, only carbon in an "allotropic" form. There seems to be a similar allotropy working in human nature. Some men seem to have all the constituents of genius, but they never reach very far above the plane of the commonplace. They are like the diamond,—except that they are more like the charcoal.

I wish to describe to you a teacher who was not a genius, and yet who possessed certain qualities that I should abstract and appropriate if I were to construct in my imagination an ideal teacher. I first met this man five years ago out in the mountain country. I can recall the occasion with the most vivid distinctness. It was a sparkling morning, in middle May. The valley was just beginning to green a little under the influence of the lengthening days, but on the surrounding mountains the snow line still hung low. I had just settled down to my morning's work when word was brought that a visitor wished to see me, and a moment later he was shown into the office. He was tall and straight, with square shoulders and a deep chest. His hair was gray, and a rather long white beard added to the effect of age, but detracted not an iota from the evidences of strength and vigor. He had the look of a Westerner,—of a man who had lived much of his life in the open. There was a ruggedness about him, a sturdy strength that told of many a day's toil along the trail, and many a night's sleep under the stars.

In a few words he stated the purpose of his visit. He simply wished to do what half a hundred others in the course of the year had entered that office for the purpose of doing. He wished to enroll as a student in the college and to prepare himself for a teacher. This was not ordinarily a startling request, but hitherto it had been made only by those who were just starting out on the highroad of life. Here was a man advanced in years. He told me that he was sixty-five, and sixty-five in that country meant old age; for the region had but recently been settled, and most of the people were either young or middle-aged. The only old men in the country were the few surviving pioneers,—men who had come in away back in the early days of the mining fever, long before the advent of the railroad. They had trekked across the plains from Omaha, and up through the mountainous passes of the Oregon trail; or, a little later, they had come by steamboat from St. Louis up the twelve-hundred-mile stretch of the Missouri until their progress had been stopped by the Great Falls in the very foothills of the Rockies. What heroes were these gray-beards of the mountains! What possibilities in knowing them, of listening to the recounting of tales of the early days,—of running fights with the Indians on the plains, of ambushments by desperadoes in the mountain passes, of the lurid life of the early mining camps, and the desperate deeds of the Vigilantes! And here, before me, was a man of that type. You could read the main facts of his history in the very lines of his face. And this man—one of that small band whom the whole country united to honor—this man wanted to become a student,—to sit among adolescent boys and girls, listening to the lectures and discussions of instructors who were babes in arms when he was a man of middle life.

But there was no doubt of his determination. With the eagerness of a boy, he outlined his plan to me; and in doing this, he told me the story of his life,—just the barest facts to let me know that he was not a man to do things half-heartedly, or to drop a project until he had carried it through either to a successful issue, or to indisputable defeat.

And what a life that man had lived! He had been a youth of promise, keen of intelligence and quick of wit. He had spent two years at a college in the Middle West back in the early sixties. He had left his course uncompleted to enter the army, and he had followed the fortunes of war through the latter part of the great rebellion. At the close of the war he went West. He farmed in Kansas until the drought and the grasshoppers urged him on. He joined the first surveying party that picked out the line of the transcontinental railroad that was to follow the southern route along the old Santa Fé trail. He carried the chain and worked the transit across the Rockies, across the desert, across the Sierras, until, with his companions, he had—

> "led the iron stallions down to drink
> Through the cañons to the waters of the West."

And when this task was accomplished, he followed the lure of the gold through the California placers; eastward again over the mountains to the booming Nevada camp, where the Comstock lode was already turning out the wealth that was to build a half-dozen colossal fortunes. He "prospected" through this country, with varying success, living the life of the camps,—rich in its experiences, vivid in its coloring, calling forth every item of energy and courage and hardihood that a man could command. Then word came by that mysterious wireless and keyless telegraphy of the mountains and the desert,—word that back to the eastward, ore deposits of untold wealth had been discovered. So eastward once more, with the stampede of the miners, he turned his face. He was successful at the outset in this new region. He quickly accumulated a fortune; he lost it and amassed another; lost that and still gained a third. Five successive fortunes he made successively, and successively he lost them. But during this time he had become a man of power and influence in the community. He married and raised a family and saw his children comfortably settled.

But when his last fortune was swept away, the old *Wanderlust* again claimed its own. Houses and lands and mortgages and mills and mines had slipped from his grasp. But it mattered little. He had only himself to care for, and, with pick and pan strapped to his saddlebow, he set his face westward. Along the ridges of the high Rockies, through Wyoming and Montana, he wandered, ever on the lookout for the glint of gold in the white quartz. Little by little he moved westward, picking up a sufficient living, until he found himself one winter shut in by the snows in a remote valley on the upper waters of the Gallatin River. He stopped one night at a lonely ranch house. In the course of the evening his host told him of a catastrophe that had befallen the widely scattered inhabitants of that remote valley. The teacher of the district school had fallen sick, and there was little likelihood of their getting another until spring.

That is a true catastrophe to the ranchers of the high valleys cut off from every line of communication with the outer world. For the opportunities of education are highly valued in that part of the West. They are reckoned with bread and horses and cattle and sheep, as among the necessities of life. The children were crying for school, and their parents could not satisfy that peculiar kind of hunger. But here was the relief. This wanderer who had arrived in their midst was a man of parts. He was lettered; he was educated. Would he do them the favor of teaching their children until the snow had melted away from the ridges, and his cayuse could pick the trail through the cañons?

Now school-keeping was farthest from this man's thoughts. But the needs of little children were very near to his heart. He accepted the offer, and entered the log schoolhouse as the district schoolmaster, while a handful of pupils, numbering all the children of the community who could ride a broncho, came five, ten, and even fifteen miles daily, through the winter's snows and storms and cruel cold, to pick up the crumbs of learning that had lain so long untouched.

What happened in that lonely little school, far off on the Gallatin bench, I never rightly discovered. But when spring opened up, the master sold his cayuse and his pick and his rifle and the other implements of his trade. With the earnings of the winter he made his way to the school that the state had established for the training of teachers; and I count it as one of the privileges of my life that I was the first official of that school to listen to his story and to welcome him to the vocation that he had chosen to follow.

And yet, when I looked at his face, drawn into lines of strength by years of battle with the elements; when I looked at the clear, blue eyes, that told of a far cleaner life than is lived by one in a thousand of those that hold the frontiers of civilization; when I caught an expression about the mouth that told of an innate humanity far beyond the power of worldly losses or misfortunes to crush and subdue, I could not keep from my lips the words that gave substance to my thought; and the thought was this: that it were far better if we who were supposed to be competent to the task of education should sit reverently at the feet of this man, than that we should presume to instruct him. For knowledge may come from books, and even youth may possess it, but wisdom comes only from experience, and this man had that wisdom in far greater measure than we of books and laboratories and classrooms could ever hope to have it. He had lived years while we were living days.

I thought of a learned scholar who, through patient labor in amassing facts, had demonstrated the influence of the frontier in the development of our national ideals; who had pointed out how, at each successive stage of American history, the heroes of the frontier, pushing farther and farther into the wilderness, conquering first the low coastal plain of the Atlantic seaboard, then the forested foothills and ridges of the Appalachians, had finally penetrated into the Mississippi Valley, and, subduing that, had followed on westward to the prairies, and then to the great plains, and then clear across the great divide, the alkali deserts, and the Sierras, to California and the Pacific Coast; how these frontiersmen, at every stage of our history, had sent back wave after wave of strength and virility to keep alive the sturdy ideals of toil and effort and independence,—ideals that would counteract the mellowing and softening and degenerating influences of the hothouse civilization that grew up so rapidly in the successive regions that they left behind. Turner's theory that most of what is typical and unique in American institutions and ideals owes its existence to the backset of the frontier life found a living exemplar in the man who stood before me on that May morning.

But he would not be discouraged from his purpose. He had made up his mind to complete the course that the school offered; to take up the thread of his education at the point where he had dropped it more than forty years before. He had made up his mind, and it was easy to see that he was not a man to be deterred from a set purpose.

I shall not hide the fact that some of us were skeptical of the outcome. That a man of sixty-five should have a thirst for learning was not remarkable. But that a man whose life had been spent in scenes of excitement, who had been associated with deeds and events that stir the blood when we read of them to-day, a man who had lived almost every moment of his life in the open,—that such a man could settle down to the uneventful life of a student and a teacher, could shut himself up within the four walls of a classroom, could find anything to inspire and hold him in the dull presentation of facts or the dry elucidation of theories,—this seemed to be a miracle not to be expected in this realistic age. But, miracle or not, the thing actually happened. He remained nearly four years in the school, earning his living by work that he did in the intervals of study, and doing it so well that, when he graduated, he had not only his education and the diploma which stood for it, but also a bank account.

He lived in a little cabin by himself, for he wished to be where he would not disturb others when he sang or whistled over his work in the small hours of the night. But his meals he took at the college dormitory, where he presided at a table of young women students. Never was a man more popular with the ladies than this weather-beaten patriarch with the girls of his table. No matter how gloomy the day might be, one could always find sunshine from that quarter. No matter how grievous the troubles of work, there was always a bit of cheerful optimism from a man who had tasted almost every joy and sorrow that life had to offer. If one were in a blue funk of dejection because of failure in a class, he would lend the sympathy that came from his own rich experience in failures,—not only past but present, for some things that come easy at sixteen come hard at sixty-five, and this man who would accept no favors had to fight his way through "flunks" and "goose-eggs" like the younger members of the class. And even with it all so complete an embodiment of hope and courage and wholesome light-heartedness would be hard to find. He was an optimist because he had learned long since that anything but optimism is a crime; and learning this in early life, optimism had become a deeply seated and ineradicable prejudice in his mind. He could not have been gloomy if he had tried.

And so this man fought his way through science and mathematics and philosophy, slowly but surely, just as he had fought inch by inch and link by link, across the Arizona desert years before. It was a much harder fight, for all the force of life-long habit, than which there is none other so powerful, was against him from the start. And now came the human temptation to be off on the old trail, to saddle his horse and get a pick and a pan and make off across the western range to the golden land that always lies just under the sunset. How often that turbulent *Wanderlust* seized him, I can only conjecture. But I know the spirit of the wanderer was always strong within him. He could say, with Kipling's *Tramp Royal*:

> "It's like a book, I think, this bloomin' world,
> Which you can read and care for just so long,
> But presently you feel that you will die
> Unless you get the page you're reading done,
> An' turn another—likely not so good;
> But what you're after is to turn them all."

And I knew that he fought that temptation over and over again; for that little experience out on the Gallatin bench had only partially turned his life from the channels of wandering, although it had bereft him of the old desire to seek for gold. Often he outlined to me a well-formulated plan; perhaps he had to tell some one, lest the fever should take too strong a hold upon him, and force his surrender. His plan was this: He would teach a term here and there, gradually working his way westward, always toward the remote corners of the earth into which his roving instinct seemed unerringly to lead him. Alaska, Hawaii, and the Philippines seemed easy enough to access; surely, he thought, teachers must be needed in all those regions. And when he should have turned these pages, he might have mastered his vocation in a degree sufficient to warrant his attempting an alien soil. Then he would sail away into the South Seas, with New Zealand and Australia as a base. And gradually moving westward through English-speaking settlements and colonies he would finally complete the circuit of the globe.

And the full fruition of that plan might have formed a fitting climax to my tale, were I telling it for the sake of its romance; but my purpose demands a different conclusion. My hero is now principal of schools in a little city of the mountains,—a city so tiny that its name would be unknown to most of you. And I have heard vague rumors that he is rising rapidly in his profession and that the community he serves will not listen to anything but a permanent tenure of his office. All of which seems to indicate to me that he has abandoned, for the while at least, his intention to turn quite all the pages of the world's great book, and is content to live true to the ideal that was born in the log schoolhouse—the conviction that the true life is the life of service, and that the love of wandering and the lure of gold are only siren calls that lead one always toward, but never to, the promised land of dreams that seems to lie just over the western range where the pink sunset stands sharp against the purple shadows.

The ending of my story is prosaic, but everything in this world is prosaic, unless you view it either in the perspective of time or space, or in the contrasts that bring out the high lights and deepen the shadows.

But if I have left my hero happily married to his profession, the courtship and winning of which formed the theme of my tale, I may be permitted to indulge in a very little moralizing of a rather more explicit sort than I have yet attempted.

It is a simple matter to construct in imagination an ideal teacher. Mix with immortal youth and abounding health, a maximal degree of knowledge and a maximal degree of experience, add perfect tact, the spirit of true service, the most perfect patience, and the most steadfast persistence; place in the crucible of some good normal school; stir in twenty weeks of standard psychology, ten weeks of general method, and varying amounts of patent compounds known as special methods, all warranted pure and without drugs or poison; sweeten with a little music, toughen with fifteen weeks of logic, bring to a slow boil in the practice school, and, while still sizzling, turn loose on a cold world. The formula is simple and complete, but like many another good recipe, a competent cook might find it hard to follow when she is short of butter and must shamefully skimp on the eggs.

Now the man whose history I have recounted represents the most priceless qualities of this formula. In the first place he possessed that quality the key to which the philosophers of all ages have sought in vain,—he had solved the problem of eternal youth. At the age of sixty-five his enthusiasm was the enthusiasm of an adolescent. His energy was the energy of an adolescent. Despite his gray hair and white beard, his mind was perennially young. And that is the only type of mind that ought to be concerned with the work of education. I sometimes think that one of the advantages of a practice school lies in the fact that the teachers who have direct charge of the pupils—whatever may be their limitations—have at least the virtue of youth, the virtue of being young. If they could only learn from my hero the art of keeping young, of keeping the mind fresh and vigorous and open to whatever is good and true, no matter how novel a form it may take, they might, like him, preserve their youth indefinitely. And I think that his life gives us one clew to the secret,—to keep as close as we can to nature, for nature is always young; to sing and to whistle when we would rather weep; to cheer and comfort when we would rather crush and dishearten; often to dare something just for the sake of daring, for to be young is to dare; and always to wonder, for that is the prime symptom of youth, and when a man ceases to wonder, age and decrepitude are waiting for him around the next corner.

It is the privilege of the teaching craft to represent more adequately than any other calling the conditions for remaining young. There is time for living out-of-doors, which some of us, alas! do not do. And youth, with its high hope and lofty ambition, with its resolute daring and its naive wonder, surrounds us on every side. And yet how rapidly some of us age! How quickly life seems to lose its zest! How completely are we blind to the opportunities that are on every hand!

And closely related to this virtue of being always young, in fact growing out of it, the ideal teacher will have, as my hero had, the gift of gladness,—that joy of living which takes life for granted and proposes to make the most of every moment of consciousness that it brings.

And finally, to balance these qualities, to keep them in leash, the ideal teacher should possess that spirit of service, that conviction that the life of service is the only life worth while—that conviction for which my hero struggled so long and against such tremendous odds. The spirit of service must always be the cornerstone of the teaching craft. To know that any life which does not provide the opportunities for service is not worth the living, and that any life, however humble, that does provide these opportunities is rich beyond the reach of earthly rewards,—this is the first lesson that the tyro in schoolcraft must learn, be he sixteen or sixty-five.

And just as youth and hope and the gift of gladness are the eternal verities on one side of the picture, so the spirit of service, the spirit of sacrifice, is the eternal verity that forms their true complement; without whose compensation, hope were but idle dreaming, and laughter a hollow mockery. And self-denial, which is the keynote of service, is the great sobering, justifying, eternal factor that symbolizes humanity more perfectly than anything else. In the introduction to *Romola,* George Eliot pictures a spirit of the past who returns to earth four hundred years after his death, and looks down upon his native city of Florence. And I can conclude with no better words than those in which George Eliot voices her advice to that shade:

> "Go not down, good Spirit: for the changes are great and the speech of the Florentines would sound as a riddle in your ears. Or, if you go, mingle with no politicians on the marmi, or elsewhere; ask no questions about trade in Calimara; confuse yourself with no inquiries into scholarship, official or monastic. Only look at the sunlight and shadows on the grand walls that were built solidly and have endured in their grandeur; look at the faces of the little

children, making another sunlight amid the shadows of age; look, if you will, into the churches and hear the same chants, see the same images as of old—the images of willing anguish for a great end, of beneficent love and ascending glory, see upturned living faces, and lips moving to the old prayers for help. These things have not changed. The sunlight and the shadows bring their old beauty and waken the old heart-strains at morning, noon, and even-tide; the little children are still the symbol of the eternal marriage between love and duty; and men still yearn for the reign of peace and righteousness—still own that life to be the best which is a conscious voluntary sacrifice."

Printed by Libri Plureos GmbH in Hamburg,
Germany